# Love Redeemed

Unwrapping the Song of Songs

> "...as the bridegroom rejoices over the bride,
> so shall your God rejoice over you."
> Isaiah 62:5

## Philip D. Cole

ISBN 978-1-4958-0623-0
ISBN 978-1-4958-0624-7 eBook

Copyright © 2015 by Philip D. Cole

All rights reserved, including the right of reproduction in any form, or by any mechanical or electronic means including photocopying or recording, or by any information storage or retrieval system, in whole or in part in any form, and in any case not without the written permission of the author and publisher.

All Scripture references are from the ESV® Bible (The Holy Bible, English Standard Version®), copyright 2001 by Crossway, a publishing ministry of Good News Publishers. Used by permission. All rights reserved.

Published June 2015

INFINITY PUBLISHING
1094 New DeHaven Street, Suite 100
West Conshohocken, PA 19428-2713
Toll-free (877) BUY BOOK
Local Phone (610) 941-9999
Fax (610) 941-9959
Info@buybooksontheweb.com
www.buybooksontheweb.com

This book is dedicated to my small group that meets every Wednesday evening. Without their incentive to take me on a journey to study the Song of Songs, this book would never have happened. I thank them for the challenge and for their willingness to attend, week after week, and participate in the discussions.

I also dedicate this book to my wife, Carol, without whom I would not have had the full benefit of the blessings that I have received from the research that was put into this project. She is forever my beloved, a gift from God, and I am immensely grateful for the opportunity of sharing this life with her by my side.

# TABLE OF CONTENTS

| | | |
|---|---|---|
| Introduction | | ix |
| Love Redeemed | | 1 |
| Poem 1 – Kiss Me! | 1:2-4 | 27 |
| Poem 2 – Dark but Lovely | 1:5-6 | 39 |
| Poem 3 – Secret Rendezvous | 1:7-8 | 45 |
| Poem 4 – Stunningly Gorgeous | 1:9-11 | 51 |
| Poem 5 – The Fragrance of Love | 1:12-14 | 57 |
| Poem 6 – In The Forest Glade | 1:15-17 | 63 |
| Poem 7 – His Banner Over Me is Love | 2:1-7 | 69 |
| Poem 8 – Spring Fever | 2:8-17 | 79 |
| Poem 9 – Reconciliation | 3:1-5 | 87 |
| Poem 10 – Marriage Procession | 3:6-11 | 99 |
| Poem 11 – Part A – The Honeymoon | 4:1-8 | 107 |
| Poem 11 – Part B – The Honeymoon | 4:9-5:1 | 117 |
| Poem 12 – Part A – The Pursuit | 5:2-8 | 125 |
| Poem 12 – Part B – The Pursuit | 5:9-6:3 | 141 |
| Poem 13 – Surpassing Beauty | 6:4-10 | 149 |
| Poem 14 – Swept Away | 6:11-12 | 159 |
| Poem 15 – Part A – The dancer | 6:13-7:5 | 167 |
| Poem 15 – Part B – The dance | 7:6-13 | 177 |
| Poem 16 – Wishful Thinking | 8:1-4 | 187 |
| Poem 17 – Redemption | 8:5-7 | 193 |
| Poem 18 – Chastity Valued | 8:8-10 | 205 |
| Poem 19 – Monogamy Valued | 8:11-12 | 209 |
| Poem 20 – God's Final Comment | 8:13-14 | 215 |
| Appendix | | 219 |
| Bibliography | | 229 |

# Introduction

The Song of Songs is the one book out of the 66 books of the Bible that many people believe belongs in brown paper wrapping and then placed on the top shelf out of the reach of children. It is easily the only book of the Bible that people don't want to admit that they are reading.

"So, what are you reading in your devotions these days?"

"Ah…" (turning shades of pink) "Song of Songs, but just because I'm reading through the Bible and it's one of the books on the way…" Maybe you've been there?

In 56 years of attending an evangelical church, listening to sermons, attending Sunday school and, in recent years, attending small group studies, I had yet to sit in on a discussion with the Song of Songs as the text and, for sure, never an exegetical study. So, when someone in our small group, jokingly introduced the idea of studying the Song of Songs as a study topic, I wasn't surprised to see the mixed response. Some were adamant that this book had little to offer to their spiritual growth journey, others were somewhat shy about the possibility; others had some interest, but saw the topic located at the bottom 6 out of 66, commenting that "there had to be a more suitable topic". Still others had their curiosity piqued. In the end, we took the matter to the Biblical process of drawing lots. We each put our choice of study in a hat and much to our … (no good word to describe our emotional reaction), the Song of Songs won the day. The concluding argument was that we had committed ourselves to the whole counsel of God, (which is a euphemism for the Bible), so why not see what God might want to teach us in the Song of Songs? This of course was mixed with all sorts of ambivalence, and feelings of embarrassment, not to mention a little snickering. There we were, feeling a little like 13 year-olds who were about to sneak the package off of the top shelf and tear open the brown wrapper so as to take a peek into the secret topic of sex.

As the Bible study leader of the group, my feelings were mixed. For some time I had wanted to take the brown wrapper off of this book so as to gain a really good understanding of the content and its role within the line-up of the other books that make up the Biblical canon. However, since the book was so unfamiliar to me, I knew that it would be a challenge. Thirdly, how was I to present my findings without blushing? Not to mention, our group included several single women, so the study had to be more than just a discussion of sex and other marriage applications. However, the name was drawn, God was possibly revealing His sense of humor, and the challenge was on.

The contents of this book reveal the next few months of my journey. (Stop thinking those thoughts, I can almost hear you snickering) What I quickly discovered was that God, in His own divine way, had put me on a journey that seemed to take two very different tracks of study, which He then miraculously merged together into one topic in the book of the Song of Songs. I have titled this merging of the two tracks as God's revelation of **Love Redeemed**.

On one level (track), which I would describe as the surface reading of this book, I discovered a series of unconnected poems describing vignettes of a couple in love. At this surface level, the poems unveil a couple's relationship in terms of passion, using what I believe would have been very graphic metaphors in their day. On this same level there are other poems that spotlight moments within the couple's life that are clouded with emotional frustration. Both the passion and the frustration expressed through the poems in the Song of Songs make it possible for us to relate to the deep-felt emotions of the couple that are on display through the pen of the poet. Therefore, it is at this level that I have chosen to search out applications for married couples, which, if you're married, you can immediately begin to apply, to the enrichment of your relationship.

There is, however, a second level (track), which is either deeper or higher than the surface level, depending upon your perspective. It is at this second level that I open up the poems to a more allegorical understanding. For it was during my journey through the Song of Songs that God seemed to also be leading me into a deeper discovery of an area that is just as foreign to most evangelicals, known as 'Spiritual Formation'. The art of 'Spiritual Formation' is learning how to draw closer to God through the practice of praying and meditation on the Scriptures in ways that our early Christian ancestors experienced. Unfortunately, most of these ways have pretty much been ignored in the past few centuries within the evangelical community. 'Spiritual Formation' has a rather mystical quality about it, so if the truth be known, it is actually more daring in some evangelical circles to unwrap the contents of 'Spiritual Formation' than it is the Song of Songs. Before you get the wrong idea and think that I'm entering into 'New-Age' territory, which I'm not, it's important that you understand what I mean when I use the word *'mystical'*. My definition actually comes right out of the Webster's New World Dictionary, which reads this way; "adjective; Having a spiritual meaning not explained by reason or logic. ...relating to direct communication with God or absolute truth." [1]

With both of these daring studies from the Song of Songs; a) marriage enrichment through sexual intimacy along with b) Spiritual formation through ancient prayer and meditation skills, merging together from the same book study, I could now envision doing all of my research in some hidden cave. Well, if you know your Bible stories, then you would agree that I would have good company.

In regards to the second track of 'Spiritual Formation' the allegorical approach I have chosen to use is based upon the New Testament understanding that the church is the bride of Christ (Ephesians 5:22-33). By using this as a foundational teaching, I have sought to suggest that, like the couples in the poems of the Song of Songs, the believer is also to enjoy, in some mysterious way, a passionate and intimate relationship with their Savior, Jesus Christ. Therefore, for each poem/song when I draw out spiritual allegories, I also offer exercises, that will assist you in drawing closer in your relationship to God.

Many of us are familiar with the diagram that shows that a marriage, which includes God, is one where the husband and wife grow closer together as they move

---

[1] The Winston Dictionary of Canadian English, publishers: Holt, Rinehart and Winston of Canada Ltd., Toronto 1970. p. 452.

closer to God. The surface level or track 1 of the Song of Songs helps couples move closer together, especially in terms of their sexual intimacy, whereas, 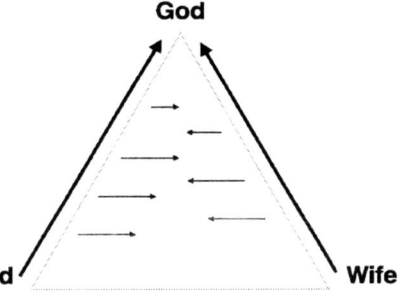 the allegorical level or track 2, helps the individual move closer to God in terms of his/her spiritual relationship. The ultimate experience for couples is that they learn to experience a true and pure worship of God through their sexual intimacy. Allegorically speaking, I suggest that sexual intimacy is a foreshadowing, in a mysterious way, of our future relationship experience with God in eternity. (Wow! Try to wrap your head around that mystical truth.) If you can't make this connection right now, don't close the book. Hopefully, this will make more sense as you progress through the remaining pages.

The layout of this book begins with a discussion of the book as a whole. I do this by providing a brief exploration of the various ways in which the book has been interpreted, but more importantly, I seek to answer the question of why God placed this book in the Canon of Scripture anyway. Therefore, the opening chapter explains the title, **Love Redeemed.** You may find this first chapter somewhat text-bookish for your leisurely reading style, but I believe that it is critical for an understanding of the rest of the book. So, please, allow me to build a foundation before uncovering the mystery of the poems. Trust me, you'll enjoy the learning experience.

After the first chapter, which discusses the message of the entire Song of Songs, the rest of the chapters represent individual poems from the Canticles. Following each poem is a research-based discussion of its symbolism, and how I believe the poem should be interpreted. After my commentary of each poem, I then offer two application suggestions. One application provides marriage enrichment suggestions and exercises for couples and the second application provides an allegorical thought for 'Spiritual Formation'. Sometimes, when the poem is longer I will provide extra marriage applications or allegorical thoughts part way through (bonus stuff), as well as at the end of my explanations. For those of you who choose to take the time to do the exercises at the end of each application, you will receive the most from this book.

I have attempted to make this book relevant to both singles and couples as a type of devotional book, or study guide for deeper discussions by offering a marriage enrichment component as well as a spiritual formation element to each chapter/poem. In this way I was able to make the study pertinent to both the married couples and the single women who attended my group. (I bet you wish that you were a part of the "in" group?) So, grab your flashlight, head to your secret hide-away and let's begin the journey.

# Love Redeemed

For our first meeting together as a group, I decided that if we were going to study a book that claims to be the Song of all songs, then a good place to start would be to answer the question, "what is the value of music?" For most people, within the western world, music has come to be an extremely important element of their lives.

Most households have vast libraries of music in digital format or on CD's, LP's, or cassettes; (probably not 8-track). Many people also aspire to be musicians in some rite of passage, like owning an instrument, (I owned a recorder in grade 5) learning to play piano at age 6, joining a choir, entering a singing competition or actually creating lyrics and melody. (How many of these have you participated in?)

It is common these days, to see someone with an earpiece that is providing them with their own special selection of music, especially someone alone on the street, on a bus or at work. The genres available in music seem to be limitless. So, why do we have such a fascination with music? What benefit does music offer mankind? I asked this question in my small group and they came up with three basic answers: A) Music helps to establish a mood, attitude or feeling; B) it provides an avenue for creative expression and C) it's enjoyable to listen to. I'm guessing that these three answers pretty much summarize our society's affection for music. Hopefully by now you have reflected on what music does from your own personal experience. Hold that thought, because it's something I will come back to, but first I would like us to reminisce over a second question.

Are you ready for the next big question of the day? What were some of the experiences and feelings you enjoyed when you first discovered that you were in love with someone? I know it's an assumption, and if you think about it too deeply, you will discover before too long that this can be a very loaded question. You guessed it; I asked my group this question as well. Song of Songs seems to be about the experiences of a couple that are passionately in love with each other, so I thought that it would be valuable to reminisce on the moments in time when your life was filled with romance. The birds were sweetly singing in the air, as you looked longingly into each other's eyes while you listened to the song of love serenading… (STOP!). Okay, you get the idea. When you come back to earth from your romantic trip down memory lane you can reflect on your answers. (Some of you are saying, "What was the question again?") The following are some of my group's answers to what feelings and experiences they remembered.

- Joy
- Passion
- Constant thoughts about the person
- Desire to serve them
- Desire to be in their presence
- Desire to communicate with them about their life
- Refreshing transparency – "I was allowed to be myself without feeling judged"
- Playful

Being able to enjoy this type of relational experience with another person is as unique to humanity, as is the creation and enjoyment of music. Some of the elements of being in love that were shared can possibly be seen in smaller and limited forms within the animal kingdom, but the full passionate package is a gift from God that is only available to mankind. As a result, all healthy human beings have a desire to enjoy, express and experience both love and music. We have this unique gift and life experience because we (humans) were created differently. We were in fact created in the image of God, and this simple fact means that love and music also speak to the character of God Himself.

As was already mentioned in the introduction, it is by God's design that our intimate relational experience be a foreshadowing of the relationship believers will someday be able to enjoy with Jesus in eternity. We experience this to a lesser degree now, but we hope to enjoy it to a much greater extent in the heavenly kingdom. Unfortunately, just when we believe that our positive experiences of romance could never end, we discover that life, with its many hardships and challenges, gets in the way of allowing our euphoric feelings and experiences of romance to carry on for more than a short time. However, it is still our hope that in our special relationships, the passion and romantic experience of love will return from time to time. Generally, this only happens when we make a special attempt to remove all other distractions from our lives. Unfortunately, in our everyday busyness this is too often a rare moment in time.

When it comes to our love relationship with God, you may believe that this dream of the return of romance (Revelation 2:4 "...you have abandoned the love you had at first.") is so far removed from reality in your mind that the best that you are willing to hope for, is to look forward to a day when there won't be any of life's distractions to get in the way of a close intimacy with God. The Bible describes this day as an eternal Sabbath. I believe, however, that the Song of Songs makes an attempt to break us away from this futuristic thinking by encouraging us to be much more focused on the relational experiences of our present lives, as they exist now on earth. This mystical experience with God, in the present and even more in eternity is to be our Song of Songs as well as, God's Song of Songs. The first verse in the book states that what we are about to read is the "song of all songs". It reminds us of other statements like the "holy of holies", "king of kings", "Lord of Lords". So, what is this "song of all songs"? I believe that it is the gift of intimacy and the gift of passion that God allows us to experience now in a small way with our beloved as a foreshadowing of the beautiful intimacy and passionate experience that God has in store for those who will one day be married to Jesus, the King of all kings.

Since working on this project, I have also met singles who have discovered this amazing romance with Jesus. In a way that goes beyond my complete understanding, Jesus has courted them, and they have fallen in love with their Savior, enjoying the same emotional euphoria that most couples experience when they discover they are in love.

**So how do we understand this book of the Bible?**

This has been a long-standing question over the centuries. For many years the Song of Songs was interpreted strictly as an allegory that described the relationship between God and Israel, with Israel being the bride. In later years, it became an allegory of the relationship between Christ and the church. This is not an improper way of looking at the book, but when we read the Song of Songs only from this perspective, I believe that it requires us to have a very panoramic perspective without focusing too much on the details. In other words, if you treat this book as an allegory, then it is important to understand this book from a broader vantage point. If you try to analyze the details of each poem allegorically, then you will find that you will miss out on the greater beauty these Songs have to offer.

Let me give you an example: if you have ever taken a dog on a hike to the top of a mountain or even a hill to see the panoramic view at the top, what you will notice is that while you are enjoying an amazing view, if you look down at Fido by your side, he will not be sitting on his hind legs taking in the view. Why, because your ability to experiencing pleasure through a panoramic perspective seems to be non-existent to Fido's nature. Fido is more likely to be found sniffing the ground or chewing on a stick. Unfortunately, by burrowing his nose into the ground, Fido is only capable of experiencing a small part of the greater picture and blessing that you are able to experience. In the same way, if you choose to use the Song of Songs as an allegory, then my warning is this: don't be like Fido who is totally focused at sniffing the ground or you will miss out on the greater panoramic view that Song of Songs has to offer. The challenge in trying to sniff out the allegorical details of the Song of Songs is that the book is all poetry and metaphors, which are not meant to be examined in the same manner as you would read a detailed instruction manual. Generally, the poet or songwriter of the Song of Songs has only one or two intended messages that he is trying to convey through each poem. He does this by the use of metaphors, similes and rhyme, so as to help us understand the significant point or statement that he desires to make. These intended messages are like the larger forests in a panoramic view. If you are studying the bark of the trees, then you could very easily miss the intended message.

Another challenge that you will find with the Song of Songs is that it differs significantly from other Biblical allegories. With other Biblical allegories there are clear references to who and what is being described allegorically. For example, in Revelation 5:6-10, there is no doubt in the reader's mind who the lamb in the allegory is. However, the Song of Songs has no such reference points, except that we can assume that God is the husband, and His people are His bride. What happens within groups of people who have tried to treat the Song of Songs as a detailed allegory is that they lack consistency with their interpretation of the described objects. For instance, the two breasts of the woman has been described by some as the New & Old Testaments, by others as the body and the soul of man, or the two commands to love God and your neighbor, and even as blood and water. There is no obvious way to interpret breasts allegorically, so it is best to allow them to be literally interpreted as, you guessed it, breasts.

Another difficulty with treating the book as a detailed allegory is that other poetry from the same time era has been discovered that uses descriptions and metaphors, which are similar to those found in the Song of Songs. However, in these other poems from the same age, there is no indication that these same literary phrases have any allegorical significance to Judaism or Christianity. Caution, therefore, needs to be taken when we seek to ascribe a sacred allegorical meaning to a metaphor when it is included in a Biblical text, but not when it is used in a secular text.

Finally, some of the described events in the Song of Songs are practices that I am told are still in use today, in the Middle East. For instance, I have read that, in some areas of the Middle East, during wedding festivities, it is common for the groom to sing a song describing his bride's perfections and her beauty (SofS 4:1-8). (I dare you to encourage the groom to try that at the next wedding you attend.)

All four of these arguments I have just listed are simply meant to suggest that if you are going to read the Song of Songs as an allegory of God's relationship between God and his people, then you need to do so with broad panoramic strokes (Don't be a Fido). After all, when it comes right down to it, all that we can clearly apply to allegory in the Song of Songs is that the church is the bride of Christ. Therefore, in some way, these poems may speak to us of God's desire for a relationship with His church and, consequently, the Christian believer, but that is probably as complex as it is safe to go.

**The Narrative Approach**

The Song of Songs is poetic and, like an onion, it has different layers of depth to speak into your life. If we read it outside of the context of poetry, we may experience a great deal of confusion and difficulty in understanding God's message in the book. One method of interpretation that can cause us confusion is by reading the Song of Songs as a narrative about a couple or even a love triangle. From a narrative perspective, the book might be read with the view that the Song of Songs is a story that describes the marriage and love life of two main characters, a country Shulamite girl and King Solomon or, you might try to read it with a love triangle variation. In this case, the plot of the Song of Songs is one of a country girl who unfortunately has caught the eye of King Solomon who, after seeing her, desires to carry her away to his harem. She, however, is in love with a shepherd, not King Solomon, so she does all that she can to resist the king's advances. These are the two different ways that the book is most often read from the narrative perspective. I believe that both ways only lead us to a misunderstanding of the true message of the Song of Songs.

Both narrative methods of interpreting the Song of Songs run into some major literary problems. The main problem is that there are no stage directions within the book, so it is impossible to know when the scene switches. Therefore, when you read the book in the narrative manner, you are left wondering at times if there are pages missing. For example, the jump in thought between SofS 4:16-5:1, where the groom is entering his love garden, and SofS 5:2, where the lover is knocking at her door but she fails to answer it, creates a huge gap between one scene and the next. Where's the page that tells what happened in the garden that has now caused her to lock him out of the house? As far as we know, the Song of Songs is not missing any of its original text, so why would it be written as if it were?

**Love Poems**

Therefore, as the lyrics of a good song are generally understood in poetic terms, the best approach to understanding the Song of Songs is to see it as a collection of unrelated love songs or poems. I have chosen, for the purposes of this book to divide it into 20 different poems. Some commentators would divide the Song of Songs into 23 or more.

The woman and the man (lover and beloved) in the poems are not to be thought of as any particular persons in real life, but should be treated as fictional characters. We will even discover that one way to view these characters is through the meaning of their names rather than understanding the names to be associated with specific people. The meanings of their names are "the perfect man of peace" and "the perfect woman of peace". With this understanding, it makes perfect sense that the author would write a series of poems or songs that would describe the perfect man and the perfect woman in scenarios which reveal love as God meant it to be between a man and a woman before their relationship was tarnished by sin. The women of Jerusalem in these songs or poems play differing roles in the various poems, as will be further discussed when I provide an interpretation of each poem/song.

As we have already discussed in the introduction, this collection of songs is poetic in nature and is filled with metaphors and similes. This genre of literature allows us to interpret the songs at different levels. For instance, on the surface, we can read the poems as a collection of very descriptive vignettes, which often describe sexual intimacy (At least it did for the people during the time that it was written). Yet at another level, the same poem may speak to us of our relationship with Jesus, whom we see as our loving Savior who will someday return for His bride (the church). It is at this second level that we may accept some of the allegorical teachings in our interpretation of the Song of Songs.

## Why is the Song of Songs in the Scriptures?

Before we begin to read the poems, let's first ask the question, why is the Song of Songs in the Scriptures? I would like to respond to this question by referring back to a suggestion already made that the Song of Songs opens the curtain to a foreshadowing of relational and emotional experiences yet to come. This is both mysterious, as Paul states in Ephesians 5:32, and mystical (it is important for you to recall the definition I am using for the word "mystical"). The writer of the book of Hebrews talks about the tabernacle, the priestly system, and the laws being a shadow of the heavenly things and a foreshadowing of better things to come (Hebrews chapters 9 & 10). We know that when it comes to our salvation, we live in the 'now' experience of freedoms, but the 'not yet', of what we trust is still to come. In other words, there is an element of our salvation that allows us to enjoy the spiritual liberties, joy and experiences that God wants for us now, but our present familiarities with pleasurable emotions and sensations are just a foreshadowing of what God has in store for us later in heaven.

## Desires and Drives

Our present pleasurable experiences tend to be related to our desires and drives that come with being human. If we were to list the longings within us that drive us and motivate us for receiving satisfaction or completeness it would soon become evident that our own personal list is similar to that of most other healthy individuals. It would also become evident that the items on our list can have both an evil and a good side. This should tell us two things. First, if these desires are common to all mankind, then they are most likely given to us by the creator of all mankind (At least this is what I believe). And secondly, if these desires can have both good and evil sides, then somehow they have likely been damaged or corrupted, probably by the fall (By 'the fall', I'm referring to Adam and Eve's committing the first Biblically recorded sin). The good news is that all of these broken or corrupted desires have been redeemed through the work of Christ.

Let's consider what some of these desires might be, and how redemption changes them:

**Security**

We all have a desire to be safe and protected. Sin, however, makes people greedy for power and wealth, which often robs others of a secure and comfortable existence. Redemption, on the other hand, offers to us salvation (Ephesians 1:7 "In him we have redemption through his blood, the forgiveness of our trespasses, according to the riches of his grace"). This salvation provides protection for our souls, so that even if our body is destroyed, we can rest assured that eternal life is ours, and that we can safely abide under the protection of God. (Matthew 10:28)

**Hunger**

A natural need and desire for everyone is to eat and drink. Without eating and drinking, we die. (No confusion there) Unique to mankind, God has built into our bodies the ability to taste and to derive pleasure from a variety of foods. Sin, however, has corrupted our liberties to enjoy food to the fullest through religious legalism, eating disorders, and abuses such as gluttony and drunkenness. Redemption, however, frees us to enjoy all foods without restrictions, but in a way that shows self-control and respect for God as provider. (Acts10:9-16)

**God Connection**

Mankind universally has sought a connection with a higher being, which he has recognized as his god. There seems to be this innate understanding within humans that there is a power that is beyond us. Sin leaves us constantly searching for this power or striving to appease a god, who leaves us struggling with a guilty conscience because of our inadequacies. Redemption, however, reconciles us to the one true God who assures us that our inadequacies are both forgiven and overlooked. Under redemption, we are able to live in full confidence of a relationship with God that allows us to draw near to Him (Hebrews 10:19-22).

**Joy/Pleasure**

Every weekend and vacation time is deeply valued as time to spend enjoying the life that we have worked all week to achieve. Tons of money and hours are spent on the search for joy and happiness. As I'm writing this, I'm reminded of a movie that is being advertised on TV in which the main plot is one man's quest for happiness. The teaser beckons us to the movie to discover if he was able to find the answer to his quest. The suggestion is that, if he can, maybe we all can. From the decision of what sofa to purchase, to what sport or hobby to engage in to what form of entertainment to watch, a major part of our lives is our quest for joy and pleasure. Sin leaves us with the belief that we are victims of injustice and life's circumstances. Therefore, we are quick to blame others for our state of unhappiness and feelings of hopelessness. Redemption, however, shows us that the path to joy is possible even when we are going through difficult times. True joy is available even when sickness, death and struggles are part of our daily lives. (James 1:2-4)

## Sabbath

Closely related to joy is what the Bible refers to as the Sabbath. We all desire times of peace, rest, sleep and harmony with the world, but sin keeps us anxious and worried so that circumstances may often leave us without the rest or peace that we crave. Redemption, however, offers us contentment and the ability to be at ease with living in our world. We are aware of wars and struggles happening around us, but we have a hope that allows us to look forward to a time of eternal rest from the hardships of life. (Hebrews 4:9-11)

## Sex

As you can see, **Redemption** is the answer to many of our desires and quests in the fallen state of our existence. There are many other drives that we deal with in life; so my list is by no means exhaustive. However, there is one more drive that needs to be discussed, and that is our sex drive. Song of Songs specifically addresses this natural God-designed drive within humanity. We don't have to be all that alert to realize that sex is very much a part of our world and in fact, once we hit puberty, it becomes a very significant part of our own life story. Wherever we turn in the western culture, the media are providing us with messages that have sexual undertones. Sin treats sex as an activity, which, if at all possible, should be void of meaningful relationship. Or, at the opposite end of the spectrum, sex becomes something dirty and unmentionable, which should be kept hidden in the dark. However, the Song of Songs teaches us about the redemption of our sexual nature, which is why I believe it needs to be unwrapped and explored. The Song of Songs is God's voice to us about God's purposes and intentions with regards to the sexual relationship between a husband and wife.

**The way God created us**

In Genesis 2:18-25, we discover several things about the perfect relationship that God created between Adam and Eve. We can assume (at least I do) that since everything that God created was perfect, that the relationship between Adam and Eve was a match made in heaven. In Genesis 2:25 we are told that they were naked and not ashamed. In my Bible training experience, I was taught that this verse is a nice way to say that Adam & Eve enjoyed unrestrained sexual union. In other words, they were free to enjoy sex in the way that God intended between a husband and wife, and so they did. Before the fall, Adam and Eve's sex life was exactly as God created it to be. It was different than what the rest of creation experienced, because sex was more than just an activity to populate the earth. Sex was designed to be part of relationship-building. It was meant to be emotionally enriching and a beautiful experience of two people becoming one, not just physically, but in purpose, pleasure, and kindred spirits. Sex was the culminating expression of their unity and commitment to each other. It allowed them to be transparently naked with each other, and yet they were not ashamed.

I checked out the word "shame" and discovered that the opposite of shame is to enjoy honor, confidence and pride. This suggests that the sexual intimacy that Adam and Eve enjoyed was honorable. Both Adam and Eve enjoyed a sense of confidence in themselves and in their bodies. If you reflect on your own sexual experience, you will likely find it fairly easy to see how a lack of confidence, honor and pride has had a negative impact on your ability to experience sexual intimacy in its fullness. It is not uncommon for a wife or sometimes a husband to be embarrassed by their body or their ability to sexually please their spouse. Adam and Eve were free from these emotional barriers.

From an allegorical perspective, I believe that the comment that they were naked and unashamed also has a deeper meaning, which can help us to understand the meaning of intimacy. In the book of Hebrews chapter 10, the author is telling his readers about the benefits of the atoning work of Jesus, which was to reconcile the broken relationship between man and God. In his explanation, he makes the following comments in 10:19-22, "Therefore, brothers, since we have <u>confidence</u> to enter the Most Holy place..." (Note: this is the place where only the priest could enter under very restrictive conditions, once a year. If you entered improperly you would immediately die, so they tied a rope around the priest's ankle in case they had to drag him out.) What this verse is saying is that followers of Jesus can now enter the most Holy place with <u>confidence</u>. (By the way, this is the place where God sits on his throne.) Let's continue: "let us draw near to God with a sincere heart in full assurance of faith, having our hearts sprinkled to <u>cleanse us from a guilty conscience</u>..." (vs.22). What we have just read is another way of saying "we have the freedom to stand before God naked and unashamed." (God sees everything, so consider yourself naked.) The amazing thing is that we can stand before Him unashamed.

Hold this thought while we go back to Genesis. Immediately after Adam and Eve sinned against God, we read in chapter 3: 7-8 that they realized they were naked and they hid from God. Obviously things had changed. So, what am I getting at? Bottom line: Intimacy, in a godly sense, is being able to stand before God, who sees all things (including our nakedness), and to stand with a clear conscience by being declared free of sin. This definition of intimacy also extends to all of our other relationships (minus the sinless part). Intimacy is the ability to be confidently transparent in a way that allows you to reveal your deepest thoughts, emotions, and desires to another person, and in doing so, remain confident that you are not going to be condemned by the person you are revealing yourself to. Wow! Imagine, the freedom to be you, without someone criticizing who you are (including yourself). This is the experience that the writer of the book of Hebrews says is ours to enjoy. We can come before the throne of God in full confidence that we will not be condemned. This is the meaning of true intimacy.

This is also far more than just sex! In our marriage relationships, we need times when we can be vulnerable and have the freedom to say things (in a non-intimidating way) that may be considered inappropriate anywhere else. We need to be able to share our fears and our desires, as well as our dreams, without having someone tell us that we are wrong or crazy or even gross. For those of you who hide behind a mask, a title, or a position, intimacy is the opportunity to present yourself 'au naturel'. As a marriage partner, you have the opportunity of giving to our spouse this gift of freedom: to invite them to be naked with their soul and unashamed, because you are not going to try to fix them, or even admonish them for such thoughts. This is the time when your silence, smile, maybe even a hug, is the best gift of all.

**But What If They Didn't Have Sex?**

When the discussion of Adam and Eve being naked and unashamed came up in our small group, the argument was raised that Adam and Eve did not experience sexual intimacy until after the fall. Apparently there have even been some teachings within Christian circles that suggested that the taking of the fruit of the knowledge of good and evil was a euphemism for intercourse between Adam and Eve. My personal belief is that it was God's intent for Adam and Eve to enjoy sexual intimacy before the event of their sin. In fact, the understanding that Adam and Eve enjoyed the purest form of sex before the fall is crucial to the premise of this book since my main hypothesis presents the Song of Songs as God's voice of redemption calling us to restore purity in sexual intimacy. I understand the Song of Songs to be a statement of how God intended sexual intimacy to be enjoyed by a husband and wife, and how Adam and Eve likely experienced it before sin entered into their relationship.

The following are four arguments that work against the probability of the argument that Adam and Eve experienced sex only after they sinned and were removed from the Garden of Eden. To start, let's return to Genesis 1:28 where we discover God's mandate to mankind, after they were created, but before their fall. In the mandate, which was given to Adam and Eve, God says, "be fruitful and multiply and fill the earth." Since it was God's intention for Adam and Eve to have children, then it makes sense that in their perfectly created state they would have a very healthy sex drive in order to fulfill God's will. The task to be fruitful and fill the earth was an enormous task for the first two to consider so it is not likely that there were any delays. If God gave you the command to make children, would you be waiting around wondering if it was okay to have sex? It would be out of God's character to allow them to do His will only after they had sinned. After all, Adam and Eve were given the choice of not sinning, so where would that leave the human race? It would be a rather challenging situation for Adam and Eve if God told them to produce children, but the only way they could do this was to first disobey God by eating of the tree of the knowledge of good and evil. Therefore, the idea that sex was their first sin is a misunderstanding of the character and the will of God.

Secondly, the phrase "and they were naked and not ashamed" comes immediately after God states his intentions for marriage in Genesis 2:24, which for those readers who see chronology of writing important, is given to us before the fall in chapter three. The paragraph reads "... and they shall become one flesh. And the man and his wife were both naked and were not ashamed." The comment on their emotional freedom to be naked and unashamed is directly related to the previous notion of becoming one flesh. Since the Bible specifically uses the word "flesh" it has always been understood as sexual intimacy. This would suggest that Adam and Eve not only experienced sexual intimacy before the fall, but that it was a completely unashamed experience. As I have already suggested, it was without shame because their relationship was totally transparent, honest, trusting and full of confidence. After the fall, they realized their nakedness and, in a symbolic way, began to hide themselves from each other because now they were no longer unashamed. They had mistrust for each other, and therefore they experienced a lack of confidence in each other and in themselves. They also experienced strong feelings of dishonor.

Another argument that some have for the idea that Adam and Eve were not sexually intimate before the fall comes from Jesus' statement in Matthew 22:30 where He states that in heaven we will not marry but that we will be as the angels. This argument suggests that Adam and Eve, in their pre-fallen state, did not have sex because in the end of time everything will be returned to the pre-fallen state. Since man, like the angels, will not have sex, then there must not have been sex before the fall.

In order to respond to this argument I would like to suggest that we need to look at the end goal of heaven. In heaven, there is no need for procreation, because all who will be there are those who have already been "born again" during their life on earth (John 3:5-7). Our current mandate, as disciples of Jesus, is to be fruitful and multiply for the cause of populating heaven. This is happening now, through the process of sharing the gospel of Christ, whereas, with Adam & Eve, their mandate was to populate the earth, not heaven. So in the redemptive state of heaven, man's purposes will be different from what they originally were at creation. The second change in heaven will be that man will not have rule and dominion, as was God's original intention for him on earth (Genesis 1:26). Instead, that privilege is given to Christ (Ephesians 1:18-23, Matthew 28:18); our role has become that of a servant (Revelation 22:3).

Finally, there is also the argument that if Adam and Eve were sexually intimate, then why didn't they have children before the fall? It would be better to say that Genesis does not record that Adam and Eve had children before the fall. We know that the Bible does not record the birth of all of their children, because Cain found himself a wife, and there are no births recorded of the daughters of Adam and Eve. Also, when God gave Eve the curse of child pain, it is stated "I will surely multiply your pain in childbearing." This speaks of an experience that would be increased and so it would be a strange comment for God to make if Eve were unaware of what it was like to give birth, and even more so, if she were unaware of sexual intimacy and the result of pregnancy. In this case, would God not simply say something like, "in that day, you will have great pain during child birth?" When we examine the curses that God gives as a result of sin, they all describe changes to their present experiences of life while living in the Garden of Eden.

I hope that the above arguments have helped us to get into the same mindset, which allows us to be comfortable with the belief that Adam and Eve, in their perfectly created state, were naked, unashamed, and enjoyed sexual intimacy in a most beautiful and pure way as God intended. However, as we know, life didn't stay that way, and so, in Genesis 3:7, we read that after they ate of the forbidden fruit "the eyes of both of them were opened, and they realized they were naked; so they sewed fig leaves together and made coverings for themselves." This is a pretty strong clue that things were no longer as they were. We can read in verse 12 that Adam began to shift blame onto Eve. Added to this, in verse 16, we also have God's curse, which describes a major change that is about to take place in their relationship. Sin has now entered the world and with it everything has changed, including sex. They were no longer comfortable in their nakedness towards each other. Symbolically, they had lost honor, pride and confidence in each other, which had allowed them to experience a beautiful relationship of transparent intimacy in all of its forms, including sexual.

**So now what?**

The question is now left for man to decide; what is he going to do about his sexual nature? Does he see it as evil and try to ignore it or suppress it? At one time, this was a message that the church commonly shared with its congregation. Does mankind create a list of taboos regarding sex or does he eliminate all of the taboos? Does he allow sex to control him or does he give it boundaries? Does he share it exclusively with his marriage partner or freely with whomever? Does he share it with the same gender or exclusively with a marriage partner of the opposite sex? Sin opened the door to many questions and diversions from what God originally intended.

In an attempt to answer the above questions, man introduced some cultural expectations, which created even more questions. So now man has to ask, "Do I allow my culture to establish what is sexually acceptable?" For instance, should a woman always stay completely covered so that a man may see his wife's hair only in the privacy of their bedroom, as is the custom in some Middle Eastern societies? Should a woman be able to prove that she can get pregnant before marrying, as is the case in certain tribal communities? Should a man be forced to marry his brother's wife if his brother dies without children, as was required in Old Testament law? Should men have several wives, as was the case with some of the Old Testament. Patriarchs? Or, should homosexuals be allowed to marry each other, as is the case in our own culture?

As you can see, culture is not a great teacher of how we should address the gift of sexuality and relational intimacy that God has given to mankind. The fall of Adam & Eve has tarnished God's original intent for human sexuality, and so mankind has, through the years, developed a complete spectrum of what he believes is alright and what is not acceptable. At one end of the spectrum, we have a very conservative stance with many taboos and restrictions that are designed to keep sex sinfully necessary for the purposes of procreation. By creating these restrictions, couples are refrained from experiencing the full blessings that God wants to provide for married couples. Many of us have been raised with a variety of restrictive messages from our own parents, even within the context of a marriage relationship. For instance, an older man in my early years of marriage told me that it was not appropriate to leave the light on when having sex. Some of you will see this as humorous and others of you will think, "Yeah, what's the problem?" There are many children who grow up being taught in their home that sex is a terrible thing and that it should be avoided before marriage. The motive of their parents is to keep their child pure for the marriage bed, but in this approach, the parents may have psychologically ruined the marriage bed experience for their child. (At least they keep marriage counselors employed). It is not sex that is terrible: God created it to be beautiful. It is the misuse of sex that is the problem.

At the other end of the spectrum, there is a very liberal perspective, which encourages excessive 'freedoms' that equally cause us to stray from God's intent. For instance, when our sexual intimacy steps out of the boundaries of being exclusively between a husband and wife, then it has become too 'liberating'.

When it comes to sexuality, each one of us has his/her own position on this spectrum. Most of us would have little difficulty placing ourselves on a graph, which charts our own sexual comfort zone between taboos and excessive freedoms. After reading this book, there is a possibility that some of your ideas may need to experience the change of Love Redeemed. You may discover that you have been too closed minded, or you may also discover that you have been too liberally minded. I hope, as you allow God to speak to you through the unwrapping of the Song of Songs, that you will be open to having God shift your comfort zone in this spectrum closer to His design.

**Song of Songs is God's voice of sexuality redeemed.**

In summary, Song of Songs answers the question of what is pure and right when it comes to sexual intimacy as God intended it to be. Once again, in the Song of Songs, the couple is presented to us, as being naked and without shame. In contrast to the curse in Genesis 3:16, which is related to the woman's desire for her husband, we have the phrase in Song of Songs "I belong to my lover and **his** desire (same word) is for me" (SofS 7:10).

We also have an allegorical message in the Song of Songs. From Luke 20:34-36, we get the idea that there will be no marriage intimacy in heaven, because we assume that this is not the case with the angels. But, what if the angels have an intimacy with God that is beyond our experience and understanding and that is much better than any sexual intimacy we can experience with our spouse? We should not overlook the marriage metaphor throughout Scripture between God and Israel and Christ and the church. Paul tells us in Ephesians 5:31-33 that marriage is to be a reflection of our relationship with God. In its purest form, sexual intimacy is the closest and most vulnerable experience a couple can enjoy together. It is both intense and euphoric in its emotional connection. Could our experience, when we make love to our spouse, be an indication of how it will feel emotionally and physically to be fully loved and accepted in the presence of a Holy God?

The Song of Songs is God's voice to us in regards to this very important part of life. It gives us permission to celebrate human love, intimacy and sexuality as part of God's perfect creation and design. The book is written poetically because sex is meant to be a creative expression of our emotional involvement with the person we love. Sex is not meant to be structured and predictable, but subjective and, at times, impulsive. God has not chosen to give us a manual of rules when it comes to sex, because, like art, he wants it to be a part of our heart's expression. The Song of Songs is therefore not a "how- to" book or a dating guide. Instead, it is meant to set the proper mood and tone for a redemptive sexual relationship. What we discover throughout the Song of Songs is that sexual intimacy is meant to be a celebration of life; it is to be both giving and respectful, and at times even playful.

Most of the love scenes in the Song of Songs take place in a garden, using garden imagery, which is in contrast to the city scenes, where the couple's relationship encounters human and non-redemptive challenges. The garden imagery throughout Scripture often represents Eden, the perfect created world of God and the place for the redeemed to enjoy God's presence, whereas the city often represents corruption and man's influence. This may be why, when Solomon designed the temple, he used garden imagery. There is also significance to the garden of Gethsemane and the cross of redemption that are both situated outside of the city walls. When you get past the gates and walls of heaven the imagery is also that of a garden (see Rev. 22). Gardens are meant to remind us of God's perfect creation.

The Song of Songs also recognizes the challenges that face lovers on this side of heaven, so it issues warnings as well as encouragements. It warns about the powerful force of love, which must not be awakened before its time. It also recognizes the importance of commitment in a relationship, even during times when the circumstances of life seem to get in the way. The book reminds us that Love must be mutually appreciated; it must also be exclusive to the couple, fully engaging and sensually beautiful. To miss out on any of these is to miss out on God's full blessing and intent.

The Song of Songs also tells us that when sexual intimacy is experienced in its most perfect expression of love, it provides a feeling of closeness with our partner that is incredibly captivating and fulfilling. In a mysterious sense, this is the same mystical feeling that God desires us to have with him on a spiritual level. When you first fell in love, much of your time was occupied with thoughts and feelings about your new relationship; God wants that same experience and attention from you in your spiritual life. As you read through the spiritual allegory sections of this book, I would encourage you to reflect on your romantic love and passions as a gift from God. They are a foreshadowing of the joy that you will one day fully experience in heaven with Jesus. You may also consider that in the now of life's journey, you can, in whatever your present situation, have times of deep joy and intimacy with Jesus through the spiritual disciplines that draw you closer to God.

It is my hope that this book will show you that the Song of Songs provides an affirmation of the joy of love and sex as God designed it to be, that it sings a song to us of God's redemption in marriage with regards to sexual intimacy. From an allegorical perspective, the book reminds us that we live in the now, but not yet, marriage metaphor of Christ and his bride, the church. By doing this, the Song of Songs provides us with a mysterious spiritual enlightenment of the relationship we can have with Christ in the now, through exercises that are commonly described as 'Spiritual Formation'. However, with all of this relationship beauty to be experienced, there is also a warning of the dangers that come with the intense emotions, that love and sex can create, so we are cautioned to not awaken love before we are ready.

With this in mind, you are now ready to venture into a new experience with the Song of Songs. I would encourage you to not read this book as you would a novel or a text book, but to read it in the way that you would a devotional book, one poem (chapter) at a time. Enjoy the poem, attempt the exercises and discover the experience of Love Redeemed.

# Poem 1
# Kiss Me!
## 1:2-4

Let him kiss me with the kisses of his mouth!
For your love is better than wine;
³ your anointing oils are fragrant;
your name is oil poured out;
therefore virgins love you.
⁴ Draw me after you; let us run.
The king has brought me into his chambers.
We will exult and rejoice in you;
we will extol your love more than wine;
rightly do they love you.

# Philip D. Cole

At some time you may have been surfing through the channels on your TV when you came across a scene where a couple is frantically engaged in passionate physical intimacy. I'm sure you know what I'm talking about: they've been out on a date, they entered the apartment and then, whoa' lots of kissing, groping and effort to get out of their encumbering clothes (of course at this point you switched the channel). The first poem of the Song of Songs leaves you feeling like you've been launched into a similar scene without any warning or preamble. Suddenly, as a reader, you feel like you just walked in on something that maybe you shouldn't have walked in on. As you read this poem, you may be tempted to say, "Excuse me," close the door and blushingly walk away. Well, get used to it. If you're going to read the Song of Songs, that's pretty much what to expect. Don't worry, the last half of verse 4 assures us that we are in good company, apparently others are also watching.

What I love about this poem is that it is so counter-cultural for its day. In the Middle Eastern culture during the time when this poem was written, women, for the most part, were to be silent and submissive. King Solomon even used his wives as a way to seal political alliances between other kings and nations. Of course he's not the only royalty to engage in this concept of marriage: history reveals hundreds of examples. Many wives were considered to be propery for the benefit of their husband's purposes. Wives were to bring beauty and domestic order to the home and eventually children, who would become heirs. One of their primary purposes was to uphold and carry on the husband's name, and provide that name with the utmost of respect.

Therefore, it is quite radical to note that part of God's message of redemption within this Song is that a wife has a voice within the relationship where she is free to express her desires. So, as is typical of Song of Songs, the woman in this poem is taking the initiative. In fact it has been calculated that the woman speaks 53% of the time and the man 39% of the time throughout the Song of Songs (of course, this is not likely to surprise most men). The other 8% are the voices of various third parties.

If the male character in this poem is indeed King Solomon, (which I'm not so sure about), imagine how daring it would be for one of his wives to be acting like the woman in this poem? It might be easier to conceptualize the boldness of the woman in this poem when you consider the story of Esther and King Xerxes. Queen Esther was afraid to even enter the king's court without being summoned, for fear of losing her life (Esther 4:11). Imagine Queen Esther entering the court with the words from this poem on her lips. Not only would it be scandalous, but it would also be life-altering for her (death). Therefore, the counter-cultural approach in this poem is both radically amazing and refreshing.

The opening line (vs.2) speaks to the power of physical intimacy. In the same way that wine has the ability to intoxicate so that we are not thinking clearly, so is the power of a kiss, but even more so, since it is better than wine. Wine was not a luxury (or sin) within this culture, but like water, wine was considered part of the sustenance of life. Water was not always available and when it was available, it wasn't always pleasant to drink. Therefore, wine was used to quench physical thirst because it had a more pleasant taste to the palate than water. So, in the same way as wine is better than water, his kiss is better than wine. His kiss provides her with sustenance to her emotions and passion to her soul, in a way that both quenches and delights.

Not only does his kiss entice her, but his cologne is equally arousing to her senses. Her comment reminds me of when men's cologne is advertised on TV. The moment he puts on the fragrance, it immediately attracts the fairer sex to drop what they are doing and run after him.

The oil in this poem would likely be referring to olive oil, which was used to rejuvenate dry skin in the Middle Eastern climate. Since oil in this culture was used in so many practical ways it was considered to be a blessing from God (Deut. 11:13-14). And so, in a symbolic way, oil was also recognized as another one of the sustaining elements of life. The poet in his opening lines is, therefore, quick to associate the sustaining blessings of both wine and oil with the blessing of love.

There may also be extra significance to the use of the phrase "anointing oil". To be anointed with oil meant that you were someone who had been given both authority and respect. In the Old Testament, the use of "anointing oil" was part of a ritual of consecration for God's blessings, meaning, to be set apart for a special office such as a priest or king. In this poem, not only is his fragrance like that of an anointing oil, but she goes ones step further to describe his "name" as being poured out like oil. The "name" of a person was a way of referring to their reputation or renown (fame). For a country where respect means everything and shame is the worst of all fates, the honor that she is giving her husband is very significant. What she is saying about her husband is that his reputation is like anointing oil, which is a statement of God's blessing and her beloved's authority. His fame and reputation are poured out like oil upon all those around him. In other words, he is a person who is well-liked, especially by the eligible young women (virgins). The picture that comes to my mind is a photo of all of the teen girls going crazy over the Beatles when they first stepped foot on American soil.

In verse 4 she calls him "king," but this doesn't necessarily mean that he's actually a king (well he could be). What I'm guessing, however, is that the poet's intention in using the word "king" was to make a comment on the social concept of submission with regards to her role as his wife within their marriage. We have already noted that the woman is the initiating voice when it comes to her desire for physical displays of affection. However, by using the word "king," she now acknowledges her husband as the lover and king, whom she is submitting to by requesting him to make the next move. She is offering him, as the king of his home, the final decision as to whether or not he will respond to her sexual desires. The woman is inviting the action of a kiss and then running to his bed-chamber, but he is the one who has to accept the invitation and then follow her initiative.

In summary, his kiss, his cologne and his fame are so powerful that her sexual desires have reached a level where she is no longer willing to wait for him to make the first move. Instead, she encourages him to run with her to the bedroom so that, in the privacy of his room, their passion of love can experience its natural fulfillment. (Any guesses as to what he chooses to do?) Wow! What a start!

The poem ends with the happy approval of the others, whoever they are. They agree that things are as they should be. (See footnote)[2] It seems strange that, when you consider the context of this poem within the Middle Eastern culture, that the poem suggests that there are witnesses, like a bunch of 'reality show' TV viewers who are watching what is happening and giving approval. Who are these people? If we are talking about marriage enrichment, maybe the witnesses are family and friends, who approve of the relationship. However, if we are reading this from a more spiritual allegory, then the witnesses may just as likely be the triune God. Whatever the case is, the message is clear that the sexual activities of the lover and the beloved have been endorsed.

The character of the husband is also endorsed. The use of the word "you" at the very end of the poem is a masculine singular and therefore it points to the husband. The meaning of the last line is that the male representative in this poem has been proclaimed worthy of love.

## Marriage Application (A):

One of my small group members pointed out that, like the man in this poem, it is important for husbands to work on their reputation within their family, community and jobs. A person's reputation should be like a beautiful fragrance that delights all who are within his circles of influence. It was the husband's character and reputation that encouraged the deep respect the woman and others in this poem had for him. We need to be reminded daily that when we represent the character of God by how we conduct ourselves, both privately and publically, that it

---

[2] Please note that the subtitles in your Bible that suggest who is speaking are not part of the original text. For this reason various translations disagree on who the speaker/s might be.

is one of the greatest forms of sex appeal we offer to our partner.

**Exercise:** Take the time to read Galatians 5:13-26. This passage begins with a list of character traits that we should want to destroy because these qualities are selfish and tend to ruin relationships. There is also a list of character qualities that we should want to embrace because these qualities are from the Spirit of God and tend to enhance relationships. Using both lists in this passage, write out at least one character trait, which you often display that has a negative impact on your relationship and your reputation (name). Come up with some tangible ways to work at destroying this trait. After you have focused on character traits to remove from your life, look at the list of qualities, described as the fruit of the Spirit. Choose one of these qualities that you need to work on adding to the list of character qualities, which reflect your reputation. After you come up with the quality you want as a representation of your life, then list some ideas for how you will seek to work on adding this quality to your life.

**Marriage Application (B):**

Within this poem we are able to see an interesting dance between marriage roles that couples sometimes find challenging to learn. The woman in this poem is using the art of suggestion, but then she allows her husband the ability to exercise his power of choice. If you are of the mindset that the husband should be the head of the home, then learning how to respectfully provide suggestions, which will allow him to make informed decisions, that will, in turn, be able to satisfy both of you, is a valuable skill to learn. Remember that when he has all of the data necessary to make the right decision, he has a much greater opportunity to not lose face and to actually make the right decision. If you are not comfortable with a particular option, then I advise you to not present it as one of his choices or to tell him straight up that a certain option will not make you a happy wife. If he is a wise husband, he will heed that bit of information and use this knowledge wisely.

Now if, in your opinion, your husband is always making the wrong choices, then one area to explore is the question: are you providing him with all of the data? When you provide him with the most complete insight that you have available for making good choices, then it will also provide him with more confidence in his ability to decide correctly. Too often, I hear from men that their wives seem to withhold information that would have made a significant difference in their final decision. When he makes what you consider to be the right choice, then it also increases your trust in his ability to decide what is best. So it is important to do whatever you can to help him make a decision that you can both live with.

**Exercise:** Practice full disclosure when it comes to asking your spouse to finalize a decision. I would encourage you to include the solution that you are most comfortable with, or, if you don't have a preference, make sure that you voice any options that would not please you.

**Marriage Application (C):**

When it comes to sexual intimacy, which is more to the point of this poem, the art of suggestion provides great importance as well as communication value to your husband. As his wife, your initiation through the power of suggestion provides him with the affirmation that you are still attracted to him. Many men wrestle with feelings of failure and inadequacy in all of their roles, including: friend, employee, husband and father. Therefore, when you offer invitations for physical intimacy, it goes a long way towards erasing from his mind the negative impressions he already has of himself. I have read countless articles and blogs testifying to the benefits a wife's sexual initiation plays within a marriage, benefits which extend beyond the bedroom. When a husband feels confident about himself and his relationship, then he will generally be a much more positive person around the home and at work.

**Exercise:** I would like to encourage all wives who are reading this book and who are in a secure marriage to consider initiating sexual intimacy this week. Make your husband feel like you are attracted to him in a physical way. If you would like to do an experiment, take note of changes in his demeanor after you have initiated sexual intimacy at least once every week. Don't be surprised if you discover a much more confident man, who is more inclined to assist you in whatever way possible.

**Marriage Application (D):**

This poem also speaks about praise for him. The phrase I'm referring to is "your name is oil poured out". The NIV (New International Version) talks about his name being like perfume. There are days, maybe weeks, when it is difficult to focus on praise for your husband or wife. Sometimes, when we are among friends and family, we may even tend to make comments about our spouse that are less than flattering. However, it is important to remember that spouses, like most other people, tend to fulfill the expectations that we have for them. We call it a self-fulfilling prophecy. If we expect them to fail, then guess what will happen? They will have a higher failure rate. However, if we communicate clearly that we believe in them to succeed, then they are more likely to succeed. When we are among friends and family, it is important that we don't extol or cater to our spouse's weaknesses. If we do, they will be less motivated to change their reputation and will find it easy to justify living within their weakness. After all, thanks partially to you, they have a reputation to uphold, even if it is negative. Pride is a powerful motivator for not changing, but when you show pride in the person you believe your partner could be, then it is also a strong motivator to generate the changes you both desire.

One of the ways that you may be catering to your spouse's weakness is when you try to justify their behavior among family and friends. It sounds like this: "well you know, he's a little shy..." Or, "That's how she's always been, so..." A better approach is to point out strengths, which may sound more like this: "He loves to talk about...", "why don't you ask him about...", "I love the way she...", "I really appreciated when..."

One of the reasons that we married our spouse is that we saw strengths within them that we recognized as being greater than the weaknesses we observed. When all was said and done, the scales tipped in favor of them. Therefore, it is important that, when you speak publicly of your spouse, you seek to point out their strengths and not their weaknesses (especially to the in-laws). Allow them the joy of having a good reputation (name) among your friends and family. Delight in their strengths and they will be more likely to want to delight you with their strengths.

**Exercise:** Consider the comments that you make about your spouse, even if they are made in jest. Ask yourself, "Are these comments contributing to a bad reputation?" Your spouse needs you on his/her side. And remember, their reputation contributes to your reputation. ("I don't understand what she saw in him.") So, the next time that you are with family and friends, watch what you say and seek to speak highly of your spouse.

## Allegorical Thoughts (A):

In this poem, she adores and praises her lover, and it's clear to see that his character is indeed worthy to be praised. Likewise, our lover, Jesus, is worthy to be adored and praised over all others. What better response could we have towards God, if not to praise His love more than wine?

**Exercise 1:** In the quietness of the moment, take a few minutes to list and offer praise to God for His excellent character qualities.

## Allegorical Thoughts (B):

A second allegorical thought to consider is the idea of inviting God to pour out His blessings upon you, for the purpose of drawing you closer to Him. God desires to bond with you, and although it may be hard for you to envision God physically kissing you, try to envision God physically touching you in a way that affirms His love towards you, like giving you a hug, a pat on the back or, if you're daring, even a kiss.

**Exercise 2:** Close your eyes and imagine how it would feel to experience a hug from God. Allow your mind and emotions to focus on accepting His embrace.

# Poem 2
## Dark but Lovely
## 1:5-6

I am very dark, but lovely,
O daughters of Jerusalem,
like the tents of Kedar,
like the curtains of Solomon.
⁶ Do not gaze at me because I am dark,
because the sun has looked upon me.
My mother's sons were angry with me;
they made me keeper of the vineyards,
but my own vineyard I have not kept!

As you read this poem, you will discover rather quickly that the mood is significantly different from the previous poem. This poem is not fast and passionate but instead it is solemn and reflective. The song is directed towards the daughters of Jerusalem, who in this case seem to represent the reader/listener. Why it is directed to the daughters of Jerusalem is uncertain.

Once again, as in the first poem, we have in verse 5 an interesting cultural contrast happening. Whereas in the first Song, the contrast was from the cultural expectation of silent & submissive to amorous and passionate, in this verse she is physically dark, which was not considered physically desirable, but she is lovely. Beauty in our eyes is very much established by culture, but not in God's eyes. In our North American culture, dark skin is considered to be so desirable that much money is spent on tanning and darkening our skin. However, in the Middle East, light skin is more desirable. Why, because it is the opposite of what is normal. My daughter, when travelling in China, was surprised to find that the same cosmetic companies, which sell products in Canada to make skin look darker, sell products in Asian countries to make the skin look whiter. In the Middle East, light skin was proof of wealth, it was a good indication that the fairer person was not required to work in the fields under the rays of the hot sun. The fact that this woman has had to work out in the field suggests that she is from the lower class of society, which may be further proof that the Song of Songs is not describing one of King Solomon's romances, since a king would be looking for someone from the upper class of society who was light and not tanned by the heat of the sun.

The skin of the woman in this poem causes poetical tension in that she is disappointed in how she looks, yet she still claims to have beauty. This tension would suggest that the poet is indicating that she has a deeper beauty that goes below the surface of the skin. One of the tensions in relationships is to see beyond the surface beauty down into the deeper inner beauty of the soul.

The contrast between her being dark yet lovely is compared to the tents of Kedar that are from the tribe of Ishmael, versus the curtains of Solomon. The meaning of the word "Kedarites" is "the dark ones" who were also enemies of Israel. Their tents were made of black goat skins. The poet compares the dark goat skin tents of Israel's enemy to the curtains of King Solomon, who is the King of Israel. Since Solomon is a wealthy king who built a beautiful temple and palace, we can assume that the curtain of Solomon is ornately embroidered and attractive. Solomon's curtain would not be on the outside, exposed to the elements, as it would be made of more fragile materials that are meant to be protected from the elements. On the other hand, the black goat skins of the Kedarite tents are rugged and exposed to the weather, in the same way as her skin.

So, we see some significant contrasts happening: wealth of king versus subsistence of nomad, temporary tent versus the solid structure of a palace or temple, a curtain designed for opulence and beauty versus a tent covering designed for protection and function, a covering designed for the inside, which requires protection versus a covering designed for the outside, which provides protection. Finally, there are the two people groups who are enemies to each other. As a woman who works the fields, she has similar contrasts. Her exterior is like the tents of the Kedarites but her interior is beautiful like the curtain of Solomon.

The Garden of Eden was no longer available to mankind as a delightful place to work; things were different under the curse. Part of Adam's curse was that his sin would require him to have to work in the fields by the sweat of his brow. As we can see in this poem, the woman is also a victim of this curse: she too has been subjected to working the fields in the heat of the sun. The angry brothers may represent the laws and restrictions of society that are not necessarily part of God's intent, or they may also be the natural circumstances of living in a sinful world. One of her brothers may even be called Murphy. The reality of life, for most people, is that it is difficult and filled with many challenges, which keep us from being able to attend to our own needs in the way that we would if circumstances were different.

In the last half of this verse, we have a play on words. She had to guard the literal vineyards while working in the fields, but as a result, she was not able to guard the vineyard of her body from the effects of the sun. This is our first introduction to the metaphor of the vineyard being used to describe the woman's body. This same metaphor comes up again in poem 19.

## Marriage Application:

It is refreshing that a book, which is primarily about sexual intimacy, known to the Greeks as "Eros" love, addresses the fact early in the book that love needs to be more than skin deep. Within each one of us, there is an interesting contrast between beauty and darkness. Unfortunately, due to the messages we hear from the media and each other, we are often only capable of seeing the darkness. People who are capable of revealing a lot of inner beauty are often passed by because their exterior beauty does not measure up to our cultural standards of attractiveness. Love Redeemed allows the inner beauty to out-shine the outer beauty. Therefore, it is important to encourage our partner by words and actions that show that we see beyond their exterior to their inner beauty. For the most part, our wives get this. Most men have only to look in the mirror to realize that their wives see the beauty somewhere deeper than what their exterior represents. Men, however, tend to praise their wives' external beauty and forget about admiring the beautiful person who resides under that radiant skin. All praise is important, guys, but it would bless your wife greatly if you would focus equal attention on her character qualities. Your wife already faces a lot of social pressure to be the most attractive person possible. For some women, this stress creates a significant burden. So make sure that she knows that you love her for more than her pretty face.

**Exercise:** Create a list of all the beautiful character traits and strengths that your partner offers. Also create a list of the many routine things your spouse does, which you often take for granted. After you have composed this list, go somewhere on a quiet date where the two of you can be alone in your own space, and share your lists with each other. Afterwards, continue to keep your list close at hand. During those times when you don't see your partner as very beautiful, reread the list to remind yourself of their deeper beauty.

## Allegorical Thoughts

In this poem we are brought face to face with the contrast that is alive within each one of us. Some parts of our lives are dark like the tents of Kedar, while other parts of our lives are beautiful like the curtain of Solomon. In this way, we are all dark, but lovely. Sinful, yet redeemed. In 1 Samuel 15:7, the prophet Samuel is in the process of selecting a king to replace Saul. His initial response is to select Eliab, but God makes the following statement to Samuel, "Do not look on his appearance or on the height of his stature, because I have rejected him. For the Lord sees not as man sees: man looks on the outward appearance, but the Lord looks on the heart." As we know, David was the one who was selected to become the next king. Throughout David's life, even though he made some major mistakes, he continued to demonstrate a heart for God, which God honoured.

**Exercise:** Spend some time in quietness thanking God that He who looks upon the heart, has cleansed and redeemed your heart for His purposes. Reflect on the fact that He is making you into a new creation from the inside out. Consider the character transformations that God has been bringing about in your life. Character beauty is actually better than physical beauty in that your character can actually become more beautiful while it matures and ages. True transformation is possible, not by masking the face with make-up, but by developing a new perspective. Romans 12:2 tells us that when we change our thoughts, we change our person. Choose today to work on a character quality in your life that could use a major make-over. Make a plan, and then find someone who will hold you accountable to your plan.

# Poem 3
## Secret Rendezvous
## 1:7-8

Tell me, you whom my soul loves,
where you pasture your flock,
where you make it lie down at noon;
for why should I be like one who veils herself
beside the flocks of your companions?
⁸ If you do not know,
O most beautiful among women,
follow in the tracks of the flock,
and pasture your young goats
beside the shepherds' tents.

One commentator sees this poem as describing a playful tease that involves a romantic rendezvous.[3] The woman begins by asking where she can find the one "whom [her] soul loves" for the purpose of having a secret time alone. His response is also a tease. He doesn't give her an exact location, but encourages her to play the game, by pretending to be a shepherdess. In this way he will be able to pursue and find her.

Veils in Middle Eastern culture, at the time that this poem was written, were not as common as they are today in the Middle East. They were worn at weddings and also when women wanted to hide their identity and remain anonymous. Prostitutes, for example, would wear a veil. In the culture of this poem, it is important that she not present herself as a woman who is chasing after a man, for this would be considered as improper as soliciting her body like a prostitute. However, the tugging voice of her love and the power of love for the shepherd tempt her to want to pursue him. Therefore, if she is to follow the cry of her heart, she must do so in disguise. Her comment is that she doesn't want to be someone who has to hide behind a veil. It would be so much easier if she could openly express her love without feeling shamed by the community.

Therefore, the situation in this poem is that she would like to get together with her lover, but she doesn't want to be hassled or teased by his peers, or worse, receive a bad reputation. Seeking him out could become very embarrassing for her, and to pursue him could easily put her reputation of purity and innocence in jeopardy.

---

[3] Tremper Longman III, *The New International Commentary on the Old Testament – Song of Songs* (Grand Rapids: Eerdmans, 2001) p.99.

However, the power of love provides a strong desire for her to be together with him and so she is willing to take some risks. His solution is for her to pretend that she is one of his colleagues. This will make it easy and natural for him to find her and, in doing so, everything will be perceived to be as it should be. By following his plan of secrecy and disguise they hope to be able to get away with out drawing attention to their relationship.

As a side note, this poem offers another argument against the idea that the Song of Songs is a description of one of Solomon's marriages. Although his father David was a shepherd, King Solomon grew up in a palace and would not have experienced life as a shepherd, especially after taking over the king's throne.

**Marriage Application:**

I am so thankful that in our North American culture we are allowed to express openly our love for each other (with some obvious boundaries). The benefit to relationship happiness is greatly enhanced by the ability to share and receive publicly acceptable displays of affection, such as holding hands, smiles of admiration and hugs, even kisses. Women, especially, thrive on being acknowledged as the special person in their man's life.

The question I need to ask men at this point is, "In your relationship, who's doing the pursuing?" I'm not talking about asking for sex, but about relationship. Are you seeking opportunities to free up time with your wife for conversation, having fun together and creating memories with each other?

If you haven't been doing this, then there is a good chance that your wife is hiding behind an emotional veil, which she would prefer not to wear. Her veil allows her to pretend when she's around friends and family that all is great between the two of you, but it isn't. It is important that, as the hunter in the relationship, you continue to pursue your wife even after the catch has been made. Your relationship, especially in the area of sexual intimacy, will suffer significantly if, now that you are married, you choose to place your wife on your check-off list of one of your life's accomplishments. In the same way that a hunter displays trophy heads above his fireplace mantle and then moves on, be careful that your wedding picture on the mantle doesn't give you permission to move onto new focuses and other pursuits. The power of love requires continual connection time, and so a healthy marriage needs your continued focus.

Along with the concept of pursuit, marriage relationships can become very routine and mundane if they are not being worked on (boring, in fact). Therefore, it is important for couples to engage in play if they want to keep their relationship spark alive and exciting. The sense of play and adventure must always be present in a relationship.

**Exercise:** This exercise is for the husbands. Do something spontaneous with your wife this week. Ask her to meet you in someplace unexpected, or show up during her lunch hour with a coffee (assuming that she likes coffee) or go out for a picnic together (You may have to talk to her boss ahead of time). Use your own imagination to create a secret rendezvous, just to enjoy the time of being together. The point is to make her feel special, because you are the one who is creating the place and the time just to be with her.

**Allegorical Thoughts:**

We have the promise of God that if we seek Him with all of our heart that He will be found, but how we seek after God is also important. I find it interesting to note that when the woman in the poem is seeking her lover, she is asked to imitate him. The shepherd invites her to imitate him by being a shepherdess, and when she becomes a shepherdess, then her shepherd will find her. This is not unlike our calling to be imitators of Christ and to care for his sheep.

The shepherd also encourages her to follow the path of the flock and to hang out around the shepherds' tents. Staying close to other followers of Christ and the church is an important part of the process if you want to be discovered by the shepherd. If you hang out in the wrong circle of people, you lessen your chances of meeting the shepherd.

In the book of Hebrews, the Christians were being persecuted, causing some of them to begin to isolate themselves from other believers. The Hebrew writer strongly urges them to continue meeting together and to encourage each other in the faith (Hebrews 10:25). There are times when God desires to meet with us one on one, but there are also times when God wants to join us as part of a group. If we want to get close to God, we need to be prepared to follow the instructions that He provides for us in getting close to Him.

**Exercise:** If you haven't already done so, consider finding a small group of Christ followers to connect with, who are intentional about studying the Scriptures and meeting with God through prayer. It is in small group interactions that you can have the joy of hearing how others have interacted with God during the week; this will give you ideas for continuing your own pursuit. Secondly, begin looking for God wherever you go in life. If you are not sure how to go about discovering God in this way; I would encourage you to check out Henry Blackaby's book <u>Experiencing God,</u> in which he shows his readers how to discover God's presence in every aspect of their lives.

# Poem 4
## Stunningly Gorgeous
## 1:9-11

⁹ I liken you, my darling, to a mare
among Pharaoh's chariot horses.
¹⁰ Your cheeks are beautiful with earrings,
your neck with strings of jewels.
¹¹ We will make you earrings of gold,
studded with silver.

Some believe that this poem may be connected to the previous poem, but it also stands alone quite easily and it has a completely different focus than the previous song, so I have decided to treat it separately. This is a poem of admiration where the man is totally enamoured by the attractiveness of the woman. Unfortunately, with the cultural difference that we experience in North America, your wife would probably not be all that flattered if you told her that she reminded you of a mare (Men, consider yourselves warned!).

To understand the significance of the compliment to the woman that is being expressed in this poem it is important to be aware that the horses that Pharaoh used to pull chariots in battle were all stallions (sexually healthy males), not mares (which are sexually healthy female horses). As it turns out, stallions have a more aggressive disposition for battle (I'm guessing it's a hormonal thing). Therefore, the nations, which were vulnerable to Pharaoh's attacks, discovered that one of the most effective defensive methods against Pharaoh's well-trained battle horses was to set free among the Egyptian chariots, mares that were in heat. Apparently, one whiff of these sexually active female horses would completely distract the stallions that were pulling the chariots. It is easy to see how difficult it would be for an army to continue in its battle plan when the chariot drivers could not control the over powering lust that was sidetracking their stallions in harness.

So, what our lover in essence is saying to the woman in this poem is that she drives all men crazy with her attractiveness. In today's world, she is the model in the TV ads who attracts the attention of the construction workers as she walks by, eliciting a few whistles and the odd comment. Discipline is completely forgotten as she awakens the natural sex drive in the males that she encounters. Some women reading this will find this behavior rather disgusting, but I tend to believe, based on how well the sale of cosmetics and women's fashion does in the world market that, secretly or not, there is in all women, a wish to be considered attractive by the men they pass by.

In verse10, by talking about her ability to display jewelry, he offers a second way to describe her as stunningly gorgeous. According to this poem, when she wears her jewelry, it enhances her beauty. It is important to note that jewelry does not take the attention away from her so as to distract from her appearance. Rather, she is so beautiful that when she wears jewelry her physical features still remain the focus of attention. The focus does not shift to the jewelry, but the jewelry brings out the beauty in her. And, since jewelry enhances her beauty, the response is obvious: he will make her more jewelry. The idea is simple: whatever draws more attention to her attractiveness is what he will continue to do. Men have been doing this for many generations.

In summary, the focus and the objective of this poem is all about describing her physical beauty and outward attractiveness. The interesting contrast between this poem and the second poem is an indication that both poems are talking about two different people and offers further proof that the Song of Songs is a collection of poems.

**Marriage Application:**

We have already discussed in poem 2 that true beauty goes deeper than the surface skin. This poem, however, encourages men to be aware of the physical beauty of their wives. On that note, wives, it is important that you seek ways to remain attractive to your husband; after all, males do tend to be visually oriented. Therefore, it is important for you to provide a visual stimulus that creates a positive emotion. However, in saying this, you also need to keep a proper balance in how you seek to adorn yourself. You may be a gorgeous model, but if your personality is ugly, it won't be long before your personality is all that your hubby sees. In 1 Peter 3:4 it reads "...but let your adorning be the hidden person of the heart with the imperishable beauty of a gentle and quiet spirit, which in God's sight is very precious." In Peter's words, beauty should not be solely based upon one's external appearance.

Men, it is wise for you to discover ways to allow your wife's beauty to shine through her character as well as her outside appearance. To begin with, stop doing the things that bring out the worst in her. On a more positive note, encourage her to do the things that bring out her best. For example, if your wife is a nurturing caregiver and enjoys displaying her character beauty by caring for others, then it is important to support her when she finds opportunities to be that beautiful person. If she is creative, help her to embrace her creativity. When you provide opportunity for her to show off her beauty, it is like creating more jewelry for her, that reflects the inner core of her heart.

**Exercise 1:** It's time to take out the list of character beauty traits that you created for poem 2. Look over the list and consider the ways in which your partner is manifesting his/her character beauty in your home and community. Encourage them to continue to shine through these ways that allow their beauty to be reflected in other people's lives. If they are not finding opportunities to allow their character beauty to shine, then maybe it's time to have a discussion as to how you could assist them in this area. Begin by pointing out the strengths that you have observed and the blessing that they have been to others. Ask them if they like using their giftedness in this way and then look for ways in which you can open up more time in their weekly schedule for them to exercise their gifts. Often people feel frustrated because there just isn't enough time in the day to accomplish more than what they are already feeling stressed-out about. Removing some of the load from your partner may provide the freedom they are looking for.

**Exercise 2:** In my book, <u>Discovering A More Intimate Response</u>, I talk about not buying jewelry for your wife that brings a focus to parts of your wife's body that she would rather hide. For example: If she is not happy with her neckline, and you buy her a beautiful diamond necklace, then she is going to be ambivalent about wearing the necklace, because she knows that whenever she wears this necklace it will draw attention to the very place on her body that she is least pleased with people seeing. If you haven't already done so, have a heart-to-heart talk with your spouse asking them what they believe are their most attractive and least attractive physical features. Ask them if there are clothing styles and types of jewelry that they prefer not to wear. Don't forget to flip the coin and find out what they love to wear as well. Getting to know your partner in this way will provide significant data for times when you are seeking to give meaningful gifts.

## Allegorical Thoughts:

Often our thoughts are focused on aspects of our lives that we are not happy with. We spend hours confessing sins and wrestling with character traits that need to be transformed. It is not wrong to be focused on growth areas, but how much time do we spend being thankful for our strengths and the gifts that God has given to us? God has created each one of us with our own unique beauty. When we choose to highlight this beauty, then it delights our creator.

**Exercise 1:** Read Psalm 139:11-18 and consider how the words of this Psalm speak to the question of who you are in God's sight. Reflect upon the beauty that God has given to you. You may have to look below the surface, but start with your smile and friendly eyes. Take the time to thank God for both the physical and character beauty that He has given to you. Make a list of the beauty that God has developed in your spiritual character. It may look like this:

Gentleness: God has created me to be a gentle and loving person. I am easy to approach and seek not to intimidate.

Caring: God has given me a heart to care for people, which is seen in the way that I...

Hopefully, this gives you the idea of how to create your own list.

**Exercise 2:** Now that you have discovered the beauty that has been given to you, take some time to ask God to enhance your beauty. Ask him to help you find areas of spiritual service and ministry that allow you to reveal the gifts he has given to you and the beautiful character traits that you have developed.

# Poem 5
# The Fragrance of Love
# 1:12-14

¹² While the king was on his couch,
my nard gave forth its fragrance.
¹³ My beloved is to me a sachet of myrrh
that lies between my breasts.
¹⁴ My beloved is to me a cluster of henna blossoms
in the vineyards of Engedi.

In this poem, we only hear the voice of the woman. It is different from the previous poem, which speaks to his sense of sight and the beauty he sees in her. This poem now focuses on the sense of smell. It is important to realize that God wants to engage all five of our senses within our intimate relationship encounters. By using all of our senses, we can receive the most complete experience of joy. Throughout the Song of Songs, you will discover how the different poems tend to bring attention to each of the various senses and the pleasures we receive from these senses.

The couch, in this case, is likely the place where he lies down to eat. Chairs and tables for eating were not the norm. Instead, there would be a low-to-the-ground table and a couple of couches to lie on while eating. This is why the NIV translates the word as 'table' instead of 'couch'.

The 'spikenard' or 'nard' that is giving off a fragrance from the woman is derived from a plant. It is one of those herbs that are easily affordable in their natural state, so it was not uncommon for it to be used as a spice in food. However, spikenard, in its processed state, where it becomes oil, is a very expensive perfume. This is why, in Mark 14:3, spikenard is described as very expensive: it has gone through the purifying process.

It is interesting to note that in this poem, the woman describes her spikenard as giving forth its fragrance, but for the remainder of the poem, she speaks of him (the king) being a fragrance to her. So the inference is that her perfume provides him with a beautiful aroma, but it's his person that provides her with a desirable fragrance. This is a similar concept to that spoken of by Paul in 2 Corinthians 2:15-16 when he says that followers of Christ are the fragrance of life to those who are being saved.

Meaning that our presence should bring joy, life, hope and happiness to those requiring encouragement and rescue.

The woman in this poem describes her man as being like a "sachet" which is a leather pouch used to hold money, but in this case it is being used to hold the aroma of myrrh. The sachet would hang around a woman's neck and was kept secure between her breasts. (Apparently thieves also have boundaries of propriety.) A sachet filled with myrrh would provide a pleasant aroma for her throughout the day. It may have been used as a natural way to freshen body smells in a similar way that we might use deodorant or a breath mint. The word picture that is provided by the sachet image is that he offers to her a security for the things that she holds close and that have value to her. He is also in a place that resides close to her heart.

Myrrh is a gum resin that comes from a thorn tree and has a very mild scent unless heated as incense. Myrrh was also used as a spice in food and for embalming, and was one of the gifts that were given to Jesus from the magi. Oddly, myrrh is used to symbolize suffering and affliction, which is difficult to understand in the context. Maybe in love there is always a sense of heartache and desire that is never completely quenched or satisfied?

When we read verse 14, the man is compared to a bouquet of henna flowers from the Engedi. The Engedi was a beautiful oasis surrounded by dry and desolate places. In this case, then, his aroma is compared to an oasis of blossoms in the midst of a desert. If this is a contrast to the sachet of myrrh in verse 13, then the poem may be speaking of the challenge within all relationships of times when we struggle to live with our partner, (represented by the sachet of myrrh, secreting the aroma of affliction), and at other times, when we can't live without our partner, (represented by a bouquet of henna flowers blooming in a dry and desolate wilderness). Another possible way to understand this poem, (if the writer is primarily reflecting upon the sense of smell), is that he smells good to her as a spice and also as a blossom.

**Marriage Application:**

I see two possible layers with this poem. In the top layer, we have a description of the physical closeness of the couple, where they are enjoying each other's scent. However, I believe that there is a deeper layer that tells us that as individuals we have a variety of needs, requiring different ways for us to be encouraged. It is our partner's role to provide for us during these needy times. God provides us with partners who are, by his intent, the scent that gives us renewed hope or a bouquet of flowers when we are in an emotional desert. In other words, speaking metaphorically, I need to be providing an uplifting aromatic presence to my wife, especially during those times when circumstances make her feel like she is in a desert. So, in the same way that she receives a moment of pleasure from smelling a bouquet of flowers, I also need to do my best to provide her with emotional joy, especially at times when life stinks. Wives also need to be an encouragement to their husbands. Metaphorically, they need to be like a delicious food aroma that promises a great taste experience. In both cases, there is this expectation of hope and emotional distraction that we can provide for each other.

**Exercise:** Ask your spouse what sorts of things tend to cheer them up when they are having a rotten day. Keep their answers at the back of your mind, and the next time life is difficult for them, bring out the bouquet of ideas they shared with you and offer them a pick-me-upper.

**Allegorical thought:**

Like myrrh, lying between the breasts, keeping Christ close to our hearts requires us to always be mindful of his affliction on our behalf. The cross should always be our hope (Galatians 6:14-17), for it is through the cross that Jesus has made it possible for us to discover an oasis within the desert of life. I find it interesting that Isaiah 35, which begins with "The wilderness and the dry land shall be glad; the desert shall rejoice and blossom like the crocus; it shall blossom abundantly..." is the passage of Scripture that Jesus used to answer John's question, when John, who was in prison and clearly discouraged, asked Jesus to certify that he was the Messiah. By using this Isaiah passage, Jesus was telling John that he was a bouquet of henna to a nation that was suffering in a wilderness that was spiritually dry. Jesus desires to bring a fresh fragrance to your spiritual journey.

**Exercise:** Read Isaiah 35 and allow God to speak to you through the words of this passage. This is an opportunity for you to practice what the early Christians called 'ced*Lectio Divina*' meaning divine reading. In order to use '*Lectio Divina*' with this passage, you will first need to be in a prayerful attitude and in a time and place where you can feel confident that there will be no distractions. Begin by reading through the passage, and listening for a word or phrase that jumps off the page and speaks directly to you.

Read the chapter a second time. In your second reading, pay attention to how this word or phrase is specifically speaking to your present situation in life. Now read it through for a third time. On this third reading, it is your turn to respond to God. Allow yourself to fully engage your spirit with God by prayerfully expressing your deepest thoughts.

# Poem 6
# In The Forest Glade
# 1:15-17

[15] Behold, you are beautiful, my love;
behold, you are beautiful;
your eyes are doves.
[16] Behold, you are beautiful, my beloved,
truly delightful.
Our couch is green;
[17] the beams of our house are cedar;
our rafters are pine.

This poem could be a continuation of the previous poem, but I have chosen to allow it to stand on its own because the theme changes from the fragrance of love to the security of love. As discussed in the first chapter, all redemptive scenes take place within the context of the outdoors rather than within the city. Therefore the language of this poem is probably describing a romantic encounter where the two are lying down together in a forest glade.

Our poem begins with the man expressing to the woman that she is beautiful, and that her eyes are like doves. (Maybe there were doves in the clearing where they were resting?) In my research, I haven't found anyone who knows the significance of comparing eyes to doves within this culture, but throughout the Song of Songs it happens several times. If her skin was being described we might be suspicious of the influence of a particular soap company. However, since it is her eyes, our next option is to consider the possible symbolism. The dove has been used as the symbol of peace, life, love, and God's spirit. So, maybe the eyes of his lover reflect some or all of these characteristics? I will leave it to your imagination. Her response to his words of endearment is to mirror back to him that he is also beautiful (hmm, clearly they have been bitten by the love bug). What we seem to be witnessing in the first part of this poem is a typical greeting where the couple acknowledges each other with terms of endearment.

After the initial greetings, we now venture into the real subject matter of this poem, namely their relationship, which is described in home-related metaphors. Their metaphorical home uses the setting of a romantic forest glade where the meadow grass becomes a couch, and the trees of the forest provide a roof made of cedar beams and pine rafters.

The word 'couch' in this poem is also translated as 'bed'. It is a different Hebrew word than what was translated as 'couch' in the previous poem. In the previous poem the couch was used for dining at a table. It is also different from the Hebrew word which is used in chapter 3:1, where the word translated in English as 'couch' is actually a euphemism to describe a place where a couple has sexual intercourse. So, within the Song of Songs, we are introduced to 3 different Hebrew words that have all been translated as 'couch', but each has a significantly different Hebraic understanding. In this particular poem, the word 'couch' is actually describing a piece of furniture. It would have been understood as a bed that was used for sleeping; often it would have had a canopy over it and netting in order to keep out the bugs.

The translation, 'Our couch is green', should not be understood to mean that the fabric was the color green or that it was somehow organic and therefore great for the environment. The word, which has been translated 'green' is actually the word 'verdant', which means 'green', but is a Hebrew word, which is most often used to describe a pleasant, grassy meadow. So, in poetic form, their bed for sleeping is a grassy meadow (I suppose this is organic in the truest sense).

The grassy area is surrounded by trees, which provide both protection and the pleasant scent of cedar. The cedar beams and pine rafters refer to the image of strength. Therefore, the description of their metaphorical home in the meadow suggests that their relationship is comfortable, romantic and is protected from the outside forces of danger by strong cedar beams and pine rafters.

The redemption element that this poem seems to be addressing is the value and importance of trust and security within their relationship.

**Marriage Application:**

Marriage relationships are meant to offer a sense of security; vows are designed to provide legal certainty. It is important to have a marriage that is as free and comfortable as a couch in the meadow, but one that is also as secure and solid from bad weather (outside forces) as a roof of cedar beams and pine rafters. The trust factor in a relationship needs to be comfortable and yet secure. As couples, we need to find ways to provide a space where we can relax in each other's presence, with the knowledge that we have built security to protect our relationship. What this poem suggests is that marriages need to develop an environment where the couple can be at perfect peace. Metaphorically, they can even sleep in the outdoors, with the knowledge of being protected.

This is the time to ask, "How secure is your relationship?" Are there things that you are hiding from each other, or are you completely transparent with each other? If you are hiding cell phone or internet conversations from your partner, (except for Christmas and surprise birthday party purposes,) then you are walking a dangerous path. I know of a couple that would hide text messages from each other claiming that they were confidential business discussions or private counseling sessions. "Really?" Unless your mate is working for the competition, which is highly unlikely, be transparent in everything. Leave your confidential work in the work place, and free up your home for open communication. Planting seeds of doubt in each other's minds will only lead to disaster somewhere down the road. When Genesis 2 speaks of the two becoming one flesh, it refers to more than sexual intimacy, but also to a transparency that is required of all good partnership relations. If you have nothing to hide, then it should be easy for you to hide nothing.

**Exercise:** Time for another walk or coffee date. This time, ask your spouse if there is any part of your life or the marriage partnership that they would like to have more information about. If there is, then this is the time to come completely clean. Try to do this without being defensive or offended. Even if the stuff they want to know is work-related, and they won't have a clue what is being discussed, sometimes it is necessary for them to be able to see for themselves that you have nothing to hide.

If you need to disclose a sin issue, depending upon how seriously this will impact your relationship (like confessing an affair), you may be advised to see a counselor on how to best speak to your partner. You will also want the counselor to help you address the sin issue and then encourage your partner to become an accountability support. Sometimes it may even be best for that type of revelation to take place within the counselor's presence. This may be a fearful and difficult emotional journey for both of you, but when couples learn to work together on difficult life situations, it tends to have a bonding effect on the relationship.

**Allegorical Thoughts:**

In our relationship with God, He desires to give us a place in His presence where we can be at perfect peace, with the knowledge that we are protected. In our souls, there are times when we need to discover the peace of

God's meadow, surrounded by His protection. We all wrestle with fears and anxieties from time to time, so when we do suffer with anxiety, it may be beneficial to read the 23rd Psalm and envision ourselves resting in a meadow under the protective care of our Savior.

I'm reminded of the story in 2 Kings 6:15-17 where Elisha opened his servant's eyes to be able to see that he was protected by a heavenly host against the armies of Syria. The forest in our poem should remind us that we, who put our faith in God, are also surrounded and protected by his care.

**Exercise:** Jesus tells us to cast our cares upon him. Read the 23rd Psalm and envision yourself as one of the sheep that Jesus is leading to a quiet pasture by the streams of living water. As you envision yourself lying in the meadow under the Shepherd's protection, hand over to him each one of your anxieties. Allow yourself to watch him take that fear upon his own shoulders and away from your worry.

# Poem 7
# His Banner Over Me is Love
# 2:1-7

I am a rose of Sharon,
a lily of the valleys.
² As a lily among brambles,
so is my love among the young women.
³ As an apple tree among the trees of the forest,
so is my beloved among the young men.
With great delight I sat in his shadow,
and his fruit was sweet to my taste.
⁴ He brought me to the banqueting house,
and his banner over me was love.
⁵ Sustain me with raisins;
refresh me with apples,
for I am sick with love.
⁶ His left hand is under my head,
and his right hand embraces me!
⁷ I adjure you, O daughters of Jerusalem,
by the gazelles or the does of the field,
that you not stir up or awaken love
until it pleases.

It is interesting that within this poem we find references to lines from songs that we have likely sung in church. In some of those hymns, Jesus is given the name of Rose of Sharon or Lily of the Valley, which likely was derived from this passage, since this poem contains the only reference to these phrases in Scripture. However, even from an allegorical perspective, understanding these flowers to refer to Jesus is probably a misrepresentation since the two descriptions are voiced by the woman in reference to herself. We are much safer to sing "His banner over me is love" with the confidence of knowing from an allegorical perspective that this line is referring to the love of Jesus for his bride, the church.

In our yard at home we have both a Rose of Sharon bush, which is like a hibiscus flower that blooms in the late summer, and a lily of the valley, which is a smaller shade-loving plant that grows in early spring and has a stem with a row of bell shaped flowers on it. Neither one of these plants is what this poem is describing. I'm guessing that these plants were named long after the poem was written.

Sharon is a very fertile area in Israel, where the fields would be covered with all sorts of wild flowers and cultivated crops. Both roses and lilies would be growing in abundance and so any one specific rose or lily would simply blend in with its surroundings and not stick out as anything special. The intention of these two lines is, to make a comment to her lover that she feels like she is only one of many other women that he could choose from. When you look at a rose bush, there are many beautiful flowers; when you look at a field of lilies, it is difficult to focus on just one because it is the large quantity of them growing together in a field or valley that creates the beauty. This is another reason why these two metaphors do not relate to Jesus, He is not just one of many, but He clearly stands out from all of the rest. What the woman in the poem has just done by making this comment is, in our household, what we call 'fishing'. She is looking for a compliment or for affirmation. (Don't tell me you haven't done this.) Of course, being the loving husband that he is, he takes the bait and gives her a lover's rebuttal by suggesting that she is not just one of many, but she stands out like a beautiful flower among the brambles. Today we might use the expression, "she is a rose among thorns".

Of course, that kind of compliment requires a response and so, as readers, we find ourselves in the middle of lovers lathering endearments upon each other. Her reply to him states that he is also unique, and one-of-a-kind. In a whole forest of trees, (Let's pretend they are pine trees); he is like an apple tree. Not only can she sit in his shadow and enjoy protection from the sun, but she can also taste of his sweet and delicious fruit. The idea is that he is a pleasant discovery (an oasis in the desert), because among all of the other trees, he is the only one that is able to provide her with the blessing of his blossoms in the spring, and enjoyable nourishment in the fall. (I know the whole dialogue is a bit sappy, pun intended.) Once they have shared words of affirmation for each other, the poem moves on to what appears to be a date.

There are various translations to describe the type of house we have in this poem. Literally, it is a wine house, similar to a pub, but a place where they primarily serve wine. The banqueting or wine house represents a celebration of love. It provides an enjoyable outing that is meant to portray the emotions the couple share towards each other. In fact, if the newspaper was to print a headline to describe this relationship, the title would read, "His banner over me is love". The phrase suggests that their relationship is marked by 'love'. If one were to ask for a description of the relationship of this couple, the answer would be easy, "They are a couple who reflect love for each other."

Unfortunately, we all know of couples who, if we were to describe them, might evoke different words such as, "They are troubled", or "As a couple, they are struggling", or "The relationship is tense", or "Their home is chaotic" or "dysfunctional". However, in this case, the banner over the couple in this poem is 'Couple in love'. It is clear for the world to see that he loves her; after all, he goes along with her fishing for compliments and actually supplies her with words of affirmation.

Therefore, as we continue through this poem, the woman begins to describe her emotional condition as someone who is 'love sick'. (Well, who wouldn't be?) In fact, she is so enamoured by her man that she simply wants him to continue to provide her with blessings (more apples). Some of you men may know what this is like: you give your wife a compliment, and she encourages you to give her another one. Well, they're not fattening, so why not feed her a few more? In the literal reading of the poem, these compliments are described as romantic delicacies for her to eat. Keep in mind that this was written in a day before chocolates and truffles were invented, so raisins and apples were the next best thing. In essence she is saying to her beloved, "Keep lavishing me with your gifts of endearment." Emotionally, she seems to require the attention.

What most happily married men have discovered is that when they verbalize their appreciation for their wife, she in turn displays her appreciation back, quite often in a physical display of affection. Therefore, as the poem draws to an end, we find the couple in an intimate embrace, and she is comfortably lying in his arms. This may not necessarily be describing a sexual embrace, but as you know 'A' often leads to 'B', so there is a good lesson in this poem when it comes to foreplay. In fact, the lesson is so powerful that the poet feels that he needs to leave his readers with a warning.

Therefore, the poem ends with a charge to the daughters of Jerusalem. The word 'charge' presents us with the idea that these women are being presented with a warning or a strong duty and a responsibility. A similar charge is made following the ninth poem in chapter 3:5. In both of these charges to the women of Jerusalem, there is a warning that love is a very powerful force and should be taken very seriously. The emotions of love are not to be fooled with or treated as some type of game. Therefore, the power of intimate love should not be unleashed until the appropriate time.

The gazelle or doe is a beautiful deer, but it is also prey to other animals, so it is easily spooked into running away. Similarly, love is a beautiful thing, but it is also something that needs to be approached with caution. It is important that you enter into a relationship with a reasonable head and with thoughtfulness: once the emotions have been engaged, it is too late to proceed with a rational mind. Once someone has been stricken with the love bug, it is impossible to provide them with your abundance of reasons as to why the relationship won't last. (Can you guess that I'm a father?) The woman in this poem is love-sick, and so the poet gives a message of warning to the other girls to be careful not to catch the same sickness unless, of course, the timing is right.

When we get to poem 9, which is also about the emotions of love, we will see that the power of love also has its down side. Emotions in both poems 7 and 9 are powerfully strong. In poem 7, we have intense positive feelings, which are in contrast to the more negative experiences of poem 9. Both feelings, however, are created by the power of love; they also are strongly influenced by the redemption of love.

**Marriage Application (A):**

There are many times in our lives when we may tend to see ourselves as just one of many, such as a lily of the field, or a tree of the forest. And although we may feel very common, we need to be reminded that in Matthew 6:28-29, the individual lily is described as a beautiful creation of God. The times when our spouse may feel like one of many is when they sense that they are being taken for granted or unappreciated. Therefore, it is important that we recognize our spouse as a unique person who has been gifted to us by God. Our spouse needs to know that they stand out from all of the rest of the people in our lives.

As a husband, I need to make sure that by my words and actions I'm not just another man in my wife's world. I need to do and say things that make me stand out above all of the rest. Likewise, wives need to make sure that by their actions and words they are not just a lily who blends in with a field of lilies (other women). Instead, wives need to be noticed by their husbands as a beautiful lily in the midst of brambles. In other words, wives are to symbolize hope in the midst of difficulties and challenges.

God gave Adam thorns and brambles as part of his curse to work the ground. Eve, however, was given to Adam as a helpmate and an encouragement; she was to be someone who could offer to him hope and joy in spite of the hard work. Husbands: Love Redeemed needs you to separate your wife from the hardships of life. You need to see her as a blessing when life around you reminds you of God's curse. Likewise, wives, your husbands are not just to be seen as another ordinary tree. They are to be the apple tree, the one who provides fruit that nurtures you and shade that comforts and sustains you. In order for this to happen, both parties have loving responsibilities that require giving of themselves to each other.

**Exercise:** Take the time this week to do something out of the ordinary to let your spouse know they are special. Give them a card. Place thank you or Post-it notes around the home where they will be seen. Tell them face-to-face that they are the most important person in the world to you, and why. Buy them a small gift to let them know that they are on your mind. These are just a few ideas to get you started. With a little imagination, I'm sure that you can come up with your own plan. Finally, tell them that you are committed to them.

**Marriage Application (B):**

In the second half of the poem, the woman speaks of her feelings toward her beloved as love sickness. Obviously, love sickness is not a condition in marriage that can be sustained, nor should it be sustained (that wouldn't be healthy, which may be why it is called a sickness). It is, however, desirable and pleasurable in short phases of the relationship and throughout our life journey together, but it is too powerful to maintain. Stirring up these feelings is an appropriate part of foreplay and so, like hot burning embers, it is appropriate for couples to stir passionate emotions into flame on a regular basis.

On this note, it may be helpful to look at sexual intimacy from the perspective of eating. There are times when you only have the opportunity for a snack. Other times may offer a more complete meal, but then there are times when sexual intimacy should be an all-out feast. As you consider the difference between a snack, a meal and a feast, you will notice that there is a progression. A meal requires greater preparation than a feast, and a feast more preparation than a meal. A feast generally pays more attention to ambiance, and more of a time commitment is required to enjoy the occasion as you move from a snack to a feast. We live busy lives, so in reality, when it comes to sexual intimacy, snacks are likely more common than meals, but meals are important because it is unhealthy to just live on snacks. And every couple should enjoy a feast at least twice a year, if not more often. To do this will require planning by both of you, and men, it will also require you to lovingly remind yourself daily that she is in your eyes the perfect lily over all others.

**Exercise 2:** Plan within the next 3 months to have a sexually intimate feast. This should be something that you are both involved in planning. Men often think they should surprise their wives with a getaway. This rarely works well. Most wives get as much enjoyment planning for the escape as they do in getting away. They will love to tell their friends, sort out just the right clothing, dream a little and so on. So include them in the planning.

This doesn't mean that you can't bring some surprises to the event. Think carefully about how you could surprise your partner with a special blessing. Also, take the time to find or write a meaningful card of gratitude that you can offer to her for the occasion. Be romantically creative! Find a nice romantic activity that you will both enjoy together. Book a B&B or a hotel in the area, and make a dinner reservation. Plan it well, and enjoy your feast.

**Allegorical Thought:**

This poem is about the intimate relationship of a couple. It is clear to see by all observing, that "His banner over her is love". When a couple is in the early stages of their relationship with each other, there comes a point when it is impossible for them to hide the fact that they are really attracted to each other (It just glows on their faces).

A Christian chorus from the 70's states, "He invites me to His banqueting table, His banner over me is love." When others see you in your daily life, what is the impression they receive of your relationship with God? Is it obvious to those around you that you have a love relationship with your Lord and Savior?

It is equally important to remember that God wants a special relationship with each person who belongs to Him. We should never feel that we are just one among many and, therefore, not that important. Jesus makes it very clear that God pays attention to even the number of hairs on our head (Luke 12:6&7). Sometimes we take for granted all of the things that God is seeking to do for us in order to let us know how special we are. We can miss out on the beautiful sunset, the gorgeous view of fall leaves, the warmth in the air, the comfort of a great meal, and the relationships we have, which give us acceptance within our community of friends and family. All of these small things that we may overlook are God's way of blessing us. If we are too busy to notice His blessings, then it will be easy for us to come to the conclusion that we are just one of His many mice in the 'rat-race' of life. When we read Matthew 6:25-33, it is easy to see that God places high value on every person.

**Exercise:** As with all of the allegorical exercises, it's best to do this exercise alone at a time when you will be able to reflect without distractions. When you are alone with God, consider what it would be like to go on a date with Jesus. What would you do together? How would He make you feel special?

One of the exercises I give to people I coach is to plan a date with God that relates to one of their senses. Each one of our senses is a gift from God for the purpose of experiencing life. So, take a sense like hearing, and plan a date around the pleasures of sound. Enjoy the sounds of nature, the sounds of music, maybe even the voice of a great sermon. Read Scripture aloud, sing, and give praise to God, thanking Him for the gift of hearing. Experience the blessings of God through hearing, or whatever sense you choose to make the focus of your date. You may also choose to pick up an idea from the retreat suggestions offered in the appendix.

# Poem 8
## Spring Fever
## 2:8-17

⁸ The voice of my beloved!
Behold, he comes,
leaping over the mountains,
bounding over the hills.
⁹ My beloved is like a gazelle
or a young stag.
Behold, there he stands
behind our wall,
gazing through the windows,
looking through the lattice.
¹⁰ My beloved speaks and says to me:
"Arise, my love, my beautiful one,
and come away,
¹¹ for behold, the winter is past;
the rain is over and gone.
¹² The flowers appear on the earth,
the time of singing has come,
and the voice of the turtledove
is heard in our land.
¹³ The fig tree ripens its figs,
and the vines are in blossom;
they give forth fragrance.
Arise, my love, my beautiful one,
and come away.

¹⁴ O my dove, in the clefts of the rock,
in the crannies of the cliff,
let me see your face,
let me hear your voice,
for your voice is sweet,
and your face is lovely.
¹⁵ Catch the foxes for us,
the little foxes
that spoil the vineyards,
for our vineyards are in blossom."
¹⁶ My beloved is mine, and I am his;
he grazes among the lilies.
¹⁷ Until the day breathes
and the shadows flee,
turn, my beloved, be like a gazelle
or a young stag on cleft mountains.

# Love Redeemed

This poem begins and ends with the woman's lover being portrayed as a gazelle. You probably haven't considered calling your man a gazelle, but if words like "stud" or "hunk" resonate with you, then you have an idea of the sentiment she is expressing. A gazelle is freely independent, beautiful to look at, amazingly agile and capable of climbing on mountainsides. In referring to the lover as a gazelle at both the beginning and the end of the poem, the author gives us book-ends to define the beginning and the end of the poem. This is a common literary practice that can be seen throughout the Bible.

In this particular poem, we have the description of a lover (gazelle) who invites his beloved to come away with him on a romantic excursion. The nuances of the poem remind us of the spring when 'love is in the air', which we typically describe as 'spring fever'. The harsh winter is over, and now is the time to enjoy the benefits of spring. One of those benefits is that all of creation comes to life, and this of course will often evoke amorous feelings among couples. In verse 8, we have the use of the word 'leaping' which creates the spirit of a playful mood. He has a spring in his step as he moves forward to his destination. Our 'gazelle' man is seen jumping over hills and mountains, and like any superhero, he is not concerned with obstacles that might get in his way. Of course, his final destination is the place where his beloved is waiting and residing for the winter. Finally, he arrives and she notices him standing in the yard looking over the wall and, peeking through the window.

The writer has painted the gazelle as a symbol of complete freedom, whereas the woman, on the other hand, is contained within the walls of the house where she can only be seen through the window that is covered with lace or lattice. The poet has now established that there is a distinct separation between the two. There is a lace curtain or veil that stands between the lover and his beloved. Allegorically, this could represent the veil between God and man, which hung in the temple. Significantly, the veil was torn (removed) at the time of Jesus' atoning sacrifice on the cross. It could also allegorically represent any barrier that comes between you and God. Or it could metaphorically represent anything that comes between you and your partner in a marriage relationship. In whatever way you choose to interpret the poem, it is important to understand that, at this point in the song, a clear contrast has been established: he is outside and free as a gazelle, whereas she is inside and behind walls.

We should also keep in mind that the outdoors and the garden represent the freedom of Love Redeemed and the world as it is meant to be (Eden). The man therefore, invites the woman to leave the home and follow after him. Therefore, the entire message of the poem, in an allegorical sense, presents strong symbolism for the theme of freedom (redemption).

It is now the springtime of the year when there is no need to be restrained by the confines of the house. Therefore, now is the time to enjoy the outside where all is being renewed from the lifelessness of winter. Flowers are growing, music is present, and the birds are mating. In terms of the cycle of seasons, spring is the time for renewal and new life, so the poet now accentuates the concept of redemption, which brings with it a new season of life. In verse 14, 'gazelle' man continues to woo the woman to be free from the walls that confine her. He desires to see her face to face without the lace curtains or rock shadows hiding her.

In verse 15, there is a warning to catch the foxes that are spoiling the vineyard. Clearly, the foxes represent trouble. These are the problems that get in the way of enjoying complete redemption and mental freedom. The admonition in the poem suggests that it is important to deal with the issues in life, which can create barriers that restrict the enjoyment of their times together and the opportunity for the couple to experience the true freedom love offers. Once the foxes have been dealt with, then she will be able to run away with him. His attention will be fully devoted to her, and her attention will also be fully devoted to him.

Grazing among the lilies in this context probably suggests that he is contented with life. Now that she is by his side, life is good. Some commentators suggest that grazing among the lilies could also be a euphemism for sexual intimacy.[4] However, I understand the poem to be more about freedom and redemption, which speaks more to the feeling of contentment and couple closeness than it does to the idea of sexual arousal.

The poem comes to a close in verse 17 by encouraging him to play like a gazelle. The idea is to enjoy life with your partner for as long as the "day provides breath" or for as long as there is a gentle breeze and the "shadows flee", which is another way to say, " as long as the sun is shining". In a very poetic way, this poem invites us to be free of life's restrictions and worries and, as a couple, enjoy the blessings of God's creation.

---

[4] Tremper Longman III, *The New International Commentary on the Old Testament – Song of Songs* (Grand Rapids: Eerdmans, 2001) p.125. and Richard S. Hess, *Baker Commentary on the Old Testament Wisdom and Psalms* (Grand Rapids: Baker Academic, 2005) p.99.

**Marriage Application:**

If you want your marriage to stay alive and intimate, then you will have to break out of the routines of life from time to time and plan to get away together to enjoy life. Don't stay at home! There is too much at home to remind you of all of the things that need to be done. Yes, it's okay to plan a getaway in order to enhance the intimacy between you as a couple. Too often couples feel guilty about doing this because they see it as a luxury. Studies have proven that for couples to be happily married, they need to get away. Marriage enrichment is never a luxury: it is good stewardship. So, it is okay to escape the daily routines, leave the city and have fun with your marriage partner; in fact it is good emotional therapy.

**Exercise:** Men, if you haven't planned a rendezvous with your wife for a long time, then you need to plan an escape. Do something fun and out of the ordinary. If at all possible, make it an outdoors event – hiking, skating, canoeing etc.

Wives, if your husband invites you to go away and play, my advice to you is, leave your work behind and enter into the mood. The warning about catching the foxes in this poem is a good reminder to us that if we don't deal with life situations, they can destroy intimacy within our marriage. Busyness, work, children, family, unresolved issues, finances can all become foxes in our vineyard. Not all of these foxes can be eliminated before you can get away, but plan to put some of them to rest before you go. Find a quality babysitter whom you will have full confidence in leaving your children with. Have the leaky water line repaired, so that you don't worry about coming home to a flood. Leave a voice message for your clients letting them know that you are unavailable for a while. Escape with your 'gazelle' man!

**Allegorical Thought:**

It is important to remember that Jesus is our redeemer. He has come to set the captive free. In each of our lives, we have something that is hindering us from experiencing the full blessing that God wants to lavish upon us. Whatever it is, it keeps us emotionally in a season of winter, when the spring season desires to bloom forth in our lives with a newness of life. Our entrapment maybe disappointment, grief, a sinful attitude that is unwilling to forgive, or simply being tired. Before doing the following exercise, spend some time with God and ask Him to name the entrapment you need to be set free from.

**Exercise:** Read Psalm 108:1-6 and Isaiah 61:1-8. Take the time to hear God's voice calling you out of the entrapment that you are in. God wants you to feel the joy of life, and to experience colour instead of black and white.

# POEM 9
# RECONCILIATION
# 3:1-5

On my bed by night
I sought him whom my soul loves;
I sought him, but found him not.
² I will rise now and go about the city,
in the streets and in the squares;
I will seek him whom my soul loves.
I sought him, but found him not.
³ The watchmen found me
as they went about in the city.
"Have you seen him whom my soul loves?"
⁴ Scarcely had I passed them
when I found him whom my soul loves.
I held him, and would not let him go
until I had brought him into my mother's house,
and into the chamber of her who conceived me.
⁵ I adjure you, O daughters of Jerusalem,
by the gazelles or the does of the field,
that you not stir up or awaken love
until it pleases.

This is an interesting poem to have within a collection of love songs that deal with intimacy as Love Redeemed. As I mentioned in poem 7, the emotional experience of this poem is significantly different, even though both emotions are driven by the power of love. This poem represents a pattern that occurs at various times throughout the Song of Songs, such as in poem 3: absence and longing, followed by search and discovery, followed by intimacy and joy. In a sense, this is the redemption path, and it applies as much to love & sexuality as it does to God's redemption of man, where God's longing for a covenant relationship with man leads Him to send Jesus to seek man's heart and to offer restoration, which is followed by perfect joy and intimacy with God and His creation.

Love and intimacy have always had their times of challenges (at least in my world). It would be fantastic to live in a world where we know that if we are in a close relationship with someone, that we will never have any disagreements with them. Sadly, however, this is not the reality of life. For this to happen, both partners would have to be perfect. However, since my wife has me to contend with, we face relationship challenges, which, according to James 1:2-4 will eventually bring us to the perfection we are seeking. So, it seems appropriate that part of God's voice in Love Redeemed is to address the times when relationships fail to live up to our partner's expectations.

It is important that we observe in this poem that there is a special attachment that has been sealed with this couple. He is not just a boyfriend to her, but he is the one whom her 'soul' loves. This speaks of a deep commitment, where the roots of their intimacy have gone down deep into her soul. Since he has been in her bed, within the cultural context of the Middle East, it is for certain that he would be her husband.

The bed that is described in this verse is different from the other beds that have been described. This bed is a Hebrew euphemism to describe the place where a couple has sexual intercourse. She is alone in this bed and does not know where her husband is. In the context of the 'bed' euphemism, "Houston, we have a problem." This is our first indication that something is not as it should be. And, since the framework of the Song of Songs is so closely focused on relational intimacy, we cannot assume that he has just forgotten to go to bed (what hormonally healthy guy would do that?) or that he needed some space for himself.

Therefore, it is important to note how she responds. Love Redeemed does not allow her to simply lie in bed while attempting to ignore the situation or for her to permit a seed of bitterness to take root, which would create a wedge within the relationship. Therefore, she gets out of bed in order to find her lover and ventures into the streets, which she discovers are potentially dangerous. Once again, we should keep in mind that the garden represents the place where all is as it should be, and the place where intimacy finds its greatest fulfillment, but this poem takes place within the confines of the city, which is a further indication that things are not as they should be. The city walls and streets represent man's creation in an unredeemed world as opposed to God's creation in a redeemed world. The symbolism speaks further to the difficulty this relationship is undergoing, and may even allude to some sin that her husband has fallen into. The fact that the poem is vague with regards to the actual problem is useful, in that it lends itself to all types of marital situations, which cause discord within a marriage. For whatever the conflict, the poem offers the same solution; that is to pursue the person and to seek a solution.

During her search, she encounters the authorities of the city (watchmen or police), to whom she inquires about her lover's whereabouts. The fact that there are watchmen in the streets alludes to the notion of danger. Clearly, this is not a place of freedom and redemption like the previous poem, because here there is a need for those who can offer protection. You will note that, in chapter 5 of the Song of Songs, there is a different response from the watchmen than in this poem where she receives no response. We need to remember that this is a completely separate poem from the one in poem 12. The significance here is that she is willing to go to the extent of disturbing the authorities in order to find her lover and to get him back. These are the men whose job it is to see what is happening, but even their eyes have been hidden from knowing what her lover is up to, which gives further evidence that he might be sinning or doing something secretive.

Shortly after meeting with the watchmen, she does, however, find her lover, and her response is to embrace him and hold him tightly. Note that she has a choice between distancing herself, such as casting blame; Or, to act in a way that will begin to draw them closer together as a couple. Wisely, she chooses to embrace. It is important to observe the four-step process for reconciliation that happens within this poem. First, she searches to find him (pursues); secondly, she holds onto him (reinforces commitment); thirdly, she brings him to the home she grew up in (seeks family or outside support); and finally, she takes him into her mother's bed (reconciles).

It is also interesting that she takes him to her mother's home. In this culture, the marriage home would be part of his father's property, not her mother's property. In a Middle Eastern marriage, the groom would go to his bride's home to meet her and then to become engaged or 'pledged to be married', as the New Testament describes it. After spending some time getting to know his bride-to-be, the groom would then go back to his father's house for the purpose of preparing an addition to his father's home or an apartment for him and his bride to live in. When this was completed, he would return to his bride's home with a wedding procession. The procession would then return with the bride, her friends and her family to his father's home for the wedding.

I mention all of this as background for the purpose of demonstrating that there is significance to the comment in this poem that he is brought into her mother's house and then later into her bed. How we interpret that significance is uncertain. Maybe, it speaks to an area in their relationship where they need to start over at the beginning? It may also speak to the important resource of family support. When we do not know where to turn for help, we often go back to the place where we received advice during our years of growing up. For a woman, this is often her mother. Another interpretation may be related to the role a mother has in producing life. Possibly, this relationship needs a rebirth: it needs to experience a fresh beginning.

The mother's bedroom can also represent a number of different ideas. Possibly her mother's bed represents a place of security for her, as well as a place of tradition and family support. Or, the bed may represent the place where her life began, thus speaking of nurture and healing. Finally, it is a place that speaks of another reason for intercourse, which is the conception of children. Whatever the reason might be for her to bring her husband into her mother's bed, the one thing we can be sure of is that, in the Middle East, the use of her mother's bed speaks strongly of the family's approval of the relationship.

My personal interpretation is that reconciliation requires healing and nurturing. For a man, part of this healing and nurturing process requires sexual intimacy as an expression of his wife's forgiveness. Along with sexual intimacy is the need for maturity and responsibility. Sex should never be considered as simply fun and games, although that is part of it. Sex also has a powerful impact on the emotions of our spouse, as well as creating children to perpetuate the next family line.

Once again, at the end of this poem, we have the same warning that was spoken of in poem 7, to not awaken love too early, before its time. In other words, do not enter into a love relationship lightly. It's important that we do not enter into marriage, which is God's place for sexual intimacy, without the commitment required to deal with the tough stuff. Both poems 7 and 9 warn the reader not to engage in love lightly. Poem 7 warns of the power of love that can go beyond control and reason, and poem 9 warns of the commitment and responsibility of love that overrides 'Eros' and the activity of sexual intimacy.

**Marriage Application:**

It should not be too difficult to surmise what the marriage application is for this poem. The poem clearly speaks to the topic of marriage commitment and responsibility. It is realistic to be aware that, at some time in your marriage, something will take place to cause discord between you and your spouse, which may significantly impact your sexual intimacy as a couple. Sometimes, temptations and other challenges in life create a strain on the marriage commitment. When this happens, it is important that one of you pursue the other and search out a solution.[5] The normal pattern, as it is in this poem, is that one person will be running or hiding from the problem while the other person pursues relationship restoration. The greatest destructive force in a marriage is the selfish pride, which causes both parties to run in opposite directions. Pursuit comes with the cost of humility, but if a marriage in distress is going to be restored, someone has to choose to begin the reconciliation process.

It is important to note that although the woman took the initiative, family support was also required. If you have grown up in a family where, for whatever reason, you do not have the support of parents, then I would strongly suggest that early in your relationship you find an older couple to stand in the gap as supportive parents. There are many older couples within the context of a church that are cheering for your marriage and family, possibly even praying for you. Connect with a couple that you respect by inviting them over to your home or by taking them out on a day trip, and begin a marriage mentoring relationship using them as your coaches. If you have supportive parents who have a healthy marriage, and they are within your geographical location so as to be able to provide you with support, then you are very

---

[5] "…if anyone is caught in any transgression, you who are spiritual should restore him in a spirit of gentleness. Keep watch on yourself, lest you too be tempted." Galatians 6:1.

fortunate to have this valuable resource at hand. Learn to use their support.

The second thing we need to observe is that in order for her to address the situation, she needed to take some risks, and to be courageous enough to go out into the streets at night in pursuit. She even attempted to get the police involved. Desperate times call for desperate measures, and in our marriages, there are times when we need to fight for intimacy and commitment. It is not adequate to be satisfied with living together as roommates. We expect roommates to move on in life. They are only with us for a season and for the benefit of reducing living costs. So, when your marriage is reduced to the mindset of "I'm staying because I can't afford to leave, but some day one of us needs to leave," then you are no longer in an intimate marriage, but in a roommate arrangement. I am guessing that when you began your marriage, it was with the desire to have your partner be your intimate companion through life. Fight for this cause! Pursue him or her in an effort to maintain this dream, and always seek to keep a mindset that refuses to reduce your relationship to roommate status.

When she finally caught up with him, her response upon finding him is important. She did not act in a way that would create a greater distance, but she embraced him. She held him and would not let him go, until she had brought him back to a safe place. Bringing someone back to a safe place in the relationship may require both counseling and family support. Or, it may be something that the two of you can handle together sufficiently. The important thing to note is that the work is not completed until restoration has brought the intimacy of the relationship back to a safe place.

The end of this poem implies that the safe place was realized when the couple became intimately engaged to the point of choosing to make love in her mother's bed. Your mother might not go for that idea, but do what it takes to get things back on track. Keep in mind that sex for most men tells them that all is forgiven, and that everything is good and back on track. If this is not the message that you want your man to receive, then it is important to communicate to him that sex may not mean the work is over and that all has been resolved, but that you are pleased with the progress so far, and that your sexual intimacy is in anticipation of a continued effort to obtain a resolution and reconciliation. Sex may be your statement to each other that you are both committed to continuing in the effort to redeem the situation.

**Exercise:** If there is something within your relationship that is driving a wedge between your couple intimacy, then now is the time to name the wedge and begin to find a solution to the problem. During this process, there are some rules that need to be followed, which I have spelled out in chapter 6 of my book <u>Discovering A More Intimate Response</u>.[6] If you do not have the skills for good conflict resolution, then together find an opportunity to talk to an older couple you both respect, or spend the money to see a good marriage counselor for guidance on how to remove this wedge. Take the step to fight for a closer and more intimate marriage relationship.

---

[6] Philip D. Cole, *Discovering A More Intimate Response,* Denver, Colorado: Outskirts Press, 2014.

## Allegorical Thought:

If we are going to look at this poem from an allegorical perspective, then it may become somewhat challenging unless we reverse the roles. Much of the Scriptures talk about God reconciling with his lost bride. The entire book of Hosea reflects God's pursuit of the bride who goes astray. It would be difficult to find evidence in Scripture of the bride of Christ looking for God for the purpose of reconciliation. However, in Jeremiah 29:10-14, the Israelites were told that they did have a responsibility to seek out God, along with the promise that when they did seek him, he would be found. Regardless of who initiates reconciliation, it is God's will that relationships be restored, especially the relationship between God and us. If we stop to think about it, there is likely something within our lives that keeps a spiritual wedge between us and God, which prevents us from having the spiritual intimacy that God desires to have with us. If something is keeping us from a proper relationship with God, then God labels that thing as an idol. Our God is jealously protecting a covenant relationship with us. He knows that we cannot live up to our fullest potential if our relationship with Him is off track. Therefore, He seeks to destroy our idols and to call us back into His embrace.

**Exercise:** Read Psalm 139:23-24 as a prayer. If things are perfect between you and God, then there will be no need for you to go any further. However, chances are that you know of an area in your life that needs work. Name this area of your life, call it what it is: greed, fear, lust, anger, bitterness, resentment, pride, busyness, independence, lack of faith, and the list goes on. Now plan a course of action for you to begin pursuing a change this week.

Maybe this will require reading a book on how to deal with unforgiveness or anger or whatever the named sin is. Maybe it will require a visit to your pastor or a spiritual director or coach. Make the effort this month to remove the wedge, and God will honor your righteous obedience.

# Poem 10
## Marriage Procession
## 3:6-11

⁶ What is that coming up from the wilderness
like columns of smoke,
perfumed with myrrh and frankincense,
with all the fragrant powders of a merchant?
⁷ Behold, it is the litter of Solomon!
Around it are sixty mighty men,
some of the mighty men of Israel,
⁸ all of them wearing swords
and expert in war,
each with his sword at his thigh,
against terror by night.
⁹ King Solomon made himself a carriage
from the wood of Lebanon.
¹⁰ He made its posts of silver,
its back of gold, its seat of purple;
its interior was inlaid with love
by the daughters of Jerusalem.
¹¹ Go out, O daughters of Zion,
and look upon King Solomon,
with the crown with which his mother crowned him
on the day of his wedding,
on the day of the gladness of his heart.

Most commentators would agree that this poem describes the marriage procession of the groom to collect his bride on his wedding day. The normal sequence for a wedding was for the young man to travel to the home of his chosen bride, where he would meet her, spend some time in chaperoned visitation to get to know her and then, if everyone approved he would ask her to become his bride. She would at this point be his betrothed. The young man would then go back to his father's home and prepare a place for him and his bride to set up a home. When this was completed, his father would inspect the home and then give the final approval for the groom to go back to the home of his betrothed and collect his bride for the wedding. This poem appears to describe the event of a groom coming to collect his bride.

We do not know if this poem is specifically speaking of Solomon collecting one of his many brides. However, the language would suggest that it is a king. It is interesting how the Song of Songs seems to switch back and forth between possible scenarios that describe King Solomon and one of his lovers, and scenarios that describe a poorer class of people, such as a field worker and a shepherd. For instance, the poem that follows this one uses metaphors that would be more familiar and significant to a shepherd, not a king. I'm not sure why the Song of Songs is put together this way, but I appreciate this approach because it reveals the redemptive work of love and the power of love, which is unrestricted by class, race, wealth, or any other factor that cultures use to restrain the natural love between couples. Allegorically speaking, it is also a beautiful picture of how Jesus is both king and shepherd.

I find it interesting to note that this poem does not indicate who is speaking. Possibly, it is the voice of

## LOVE REDEEMED

a narrator. The song begins with a question, which causes the listener to look towards the wilderness. The wilderness never represents Eden, but is always a spiritually dry place where God tests His people. Out of the wilderness comes the arrival of someone in King Solomon's palanquin. A palanquin does not have wheels. It is a covered coach that is carried by 4 to 6 men on the front and 4 to 6 men on the back. The palanquin in this poem appears to be attended by Solomon's cohort. The poetic language seems to suggest that the bride is the Promised Land that King Solomon has broken free of the wilderness to enjoy (reflections of Isaiah 62:4-5)[7].

As Solomon's palanquin is seen coming from a distance, not only do we see a pillar of smoke in the distance, but poetic license also allows us to smell the smoke. I am not sure if incense was used in some processions, but it could have been part of the splendor of a royal entrance. There may also be an allusion to the temple and sacrifices, which offered a pleasing aroma up to heaven. We do know that myrrh and frankincense were not natural to Israel, but were imported from Arabia and India. It is interesting that these were also gifts to Jesus, but there is not likely a connection to Jesus' birth in this poem.

We are also told that there are sixty soldiers accompanying this procession. The king's guard would normally only contain thirty soldiers. However, this is an important occasion, so the force has been doubled, and, not only is the force doubled, but these are special soldiers: they are an elite group of men, well armed and

---

[7] Isaiah 62:4 *"You shall no more be termed Forsaken, and your land shall no more be termed Desolate, but you shall be called My Delight Is in Her, and your land Married; for the Lord delights in you, and your land shall be married."*

prepared for the terrors of the night. In today's army, they would be an exclusive force. This may represent the dangers and difficulties that are experienced when travelling through the wilderness, or, the entire image that we are given may be designed to speak to us of King Solomon's wealth, power and security, suggesting that this party is coming with a mission, and nothing is going to get in the way of the king fulfilling the task he has set out to accomplish. With the wilderness inference, the wedding procession is also a reminder of redemption. It is the picture of the groom defeating the enemies of life for his bride and a marriage relationship.

The palanquin, we discover, is also made to King Solomon's instruction and is as ornate as his palace and maybe even the temple. It is made with the best possible wood from Lebanon, which is overlaid with silver, gold and purple. Purple is a dye made from the Murex shellfish, which could at that time only be purchased from the Phoenicians, who were the only ones who knew how to create it. The emphasis on craftsmanship reminds us of opulence and importance. The comment that the interior was made with love by the daughters of Jerusalem may suggest that touches were added by these women to decorate it for the wedding occasion, probably not tin cans and a 'just married' sign.

When we come to the end of the poem, it is strange that King Solomon's mother provides a wedding crown, but I'm guessing that this alludes to her acceptance of the bride. It may have been a special crown that was given to any groom by his mother on his wedding day, or it could also be referring to King Solomon's natural handsome appearance.

After pondering the meaning of this poem, I believe that the final line may be the key to understanding the reflections of this song with regards to the theme of Love Redeemed. The final line states that "this is the day his heart rejoiced". It is not uncommon for weddings to be the time for families to rise above their normal life-standard. Limousines, tuxedos, evening gowns, gourmet meals and other posh and extravagant efforts go into making a wedding memorable and special to the couple and family. However, Love Redeemed reminds us that the day is not to be about the glamour, but about the couple who are entering into a covenant commitment. Therefore, at the end of this poem that describes great pomp and ceremony, I think that it is appropriate to make a statement about the groom's heart-felt feelings. This is the day his heart rejoices. King Solomon had great wealth and power at his disposal, but these were not the things that made him happy or fulfilled. A quick look at Ecclesiastes chapter 2:4-11 will vouch for that. What does, however, make his heart rejoice is the beginning of a new relationship with his bride-to-be. Relationship trumps everything else. In a day when there are many other avenues of life upon which to focus our commitments, our relationships are key.

Allegorically, this poem may simply be speaking of God's rescue. Clearly, this would not be speaking of the first coming of Christ, because there was no pomp displayed as a babe lying in a manger. However, the overwhelming power and triumphant procession may provide reference to the second coming, when Jesus comes to claim his bride.

**Marriage Application:**

In the preparation for a wedding, we have the tendency to lose focus on the central purpose of the event. During the wedding, our eyes and senses can be drawn to the opulence of the occasion rather than the significance of the vows. The wedding day should be the most exciting day of our lives when we celebrate with family and friends our entrance into a life-long relationship commitment. Anniversaries are also a great time for couples to renew their lifetime commitment to each other, but there is nothing wrong with being reminded about your wedding vows more often than once a year.

**Exercise:** This week, find a special way to tell your spouse that you love them, that they continue to make your heart rejoice and that you are glad that you are married to them. Put some effort into this moment by doing something that clearly shows that you put thought and effort into making your spouse realize that they are the most significant person in your life. If you have a video of your wedding, arrange to have your vows played, and then tell each other that you are still committed to your vows.

**Allegorical Thought:**

The most anticipated hope for Christians throughout the centuries is the day when the bridegroom will call for his bride. Earlier I discussed the process that would take place around preparations for an ancient middle eastern wedding, how it would require the groom to prepare a place for his bride and then finally, how after receiving his father's permission, he would be able to return to collect his bride. This is the language of John 14:3 "I go to prepare a place for you, that where I am you may be also". Remember that when Jesus was asked for the time of his return, he stated that only the Father knew the hour and time. What believers have understood since the ascension of Jesus is that He has gone to prepare a place for his bride (the church) and at the time when our Heavenly Father gives his okay, Jesus will return to receive his bride.

The event will indeed be a spectacular occasion for all believers, but what needs to outshine the glitter of heaven in the believer's mind, is being face-to-face with Jesus in the same intimate way as a bride is with her groom on their wedding day. Sometimes, it seems that people are looking more forward to the opulence of the place with golden streets than they are to the person the place represents. Heaven is not just a place; it is the renewal of a connection with God. Therefore, the arrival in heaven needs to be valued as the time when we will experience a face-to-face restored relationship (1 Corinthians 13:12). The question arises, what am I doing to prepare for the day when I will see Jesus face-to-face?

**Exercise**: St. Ignatius of Loyola introduced a way of praying called the *'prayer of examen'*. This is a time at the end of a day when you quietly reflect on your day and the events that took place during the day. As you reflect on moments when God was clearly present and you could see him at work around you and within your life, give gratitude and praise to God. As you consider those times in the day when you failed to live up to the expectations of your Christian faith, take the time to confess your sins and get right with God. End your time of prayer with adoration for God's love to you. Tell him that you look forward to the day when you will see each other face-to-face.

# Poem 11
## Part A – The Honeymoon
## 4:1-8

Behold, you are beautiful, my love,
behold, you are beautiful!
Your eyes are doves
behind your veil.
Your hair is like a flock of goats
leaping down the slopes of Gilead.
² Your teeth are like a flock of shorn ewes
that have come up from the washing,
all of which bear twins,
and not one among them has lost its young.
³ Your lips are like a scarlet thread,
and your mouth is lovely.
Your cheeks are like halves of a pomegranate
behind your veil.
⁴ Your neck is like the tower of David,
built in rows of stone;
on it hang a thousand shields,
all of them shields of warriors.
⁵ Your two breasts are like two fawns,
twins of a gazelle,
that graze among the lilies.
⁶ Until the day breathes
and the shadows flee,
I will go away to the mountain of myrrh

and the hill of frankincense.
⁷ You are altogether beautiful, my love;
there is no flaw in you.
⁸ Come with me from Lebanon, my bride;
come with me from Lebanon.
Depart from the peak of Amana,
from the peak of Senir and Hermon,
from the dens of lions,
from the mountains of leopards.

Tremper Longman III, in his commentary, splits this poem into three different poems (4:1-7, 8-9, 10-5:1)[8] since there are three focus shifts, which take place in these verses. However, I would like to consider it as one poem. Since it is a long poem, I have, divided my comments into parts A and B. This particular song allows the reader to share in the honeymoon experience of the couple. You may be asking the question, "Do I want to do that?" While it is true that honeymoons are intended to be private, God has chosen through this honeymoon song to open a door of discovery into His intentions for and acceptance of passionate sexual intimacy within marriage. And, since we are dealing with a fictitious couple, we might as well see what God wants to share with us.

In the previous chapter, we witnessed a wedding procession. The Song of Songs does not allow us to be a part of the actual wedding vows, but now jumps ahead to the honeymoon. It would be easy to surmise that this poem is part of the same wedding seen in the previous poem; however, the comments in this poem reflect the perspective of a shepherd, not a king. Therefore, it is not likely a poem about a king, although, who's to say that the poet wasn't a king?

The first part of this poem offers a description of the bride in what seems to be strange graphic metaphors to the western mind of the 21st century. However, it was not unusual in the Middle Eastern culture of that day for the groom to offer compliments about his bride similar to those seen in this poem. This would take place as part of their wedding ceremony, as a public prelude to the

---

[8] Tremper Longman III, *The New International Commentary on the Old Testament – Song of Songs* (Grand Rapids: Eerdmans, 2001) pp.140-159.

time when the bride and groom would enter into their private shelter to consummate their marriage. In North American weddings today, we would have a toast to the bride, which is significantly less intimate than what we read in this script.

Much fun has been had regarding the metaphors that are used in this poem to describe the bride. In fact, if we were to take these metaphors literally, we would see a picture of a very ugly bride. When initially discussing this poem with my small group I came across several pictures on-line that humorously attempt to do this, but because of copyright restrictions I have decided not to insert them. You might enjoy doing your own search by entering 'Song of Solomon's bride' in Google images. My suggestion to the men is to choose not to use these metaphors as a prelude to your honeymoon: they just don't have the same intimate impact today as they did at the time of their writing.

However, if we attempt to place ourselves into the culture of the poem, we will begin to realize that our bride is actually described as a person who the lover sees as very beautiful. The Hebrew language tends to use metaphors instead of adjectives, which may have more to do with the limitations of the language than the style of writing. The descriptions used are of those things in his life that he values and recognizes for their beauty, each in a different way, which should lead men to the question, "What do I value in its beauty that I could use to describe my wife?" As I discussed this with my wife, nothing seemed to resonate as a compliment to her, so we chose to keep our words of endearment and well-used adjectives.

The description of the bride begins with the top of her head and works its way down to her breasts. To begin at the top is very important, as the Middle Eastern culture recognizes the head to be the glory of a person and the feet to be shameful. We have already discussed her eyes, which are likened to doves in poem 6. In this poem, they are behind a veil, which in this context is likely a wedding veil. Her hair is black and wavy and reminds him of a flock of goats moving down the side of a mountain in Gilead. Gilead was a beautiful pasturing area with lots of tall green grass for the flocks to enjoy. For a shepherd, this picture of a flock on fertile grass would signify the blessings of God. I'm always amazed when I go for a drive in the country with my farmer friends at how fascinated they are by the various crops that we see along the way. I could just picture one of them describing his wife's hair as golden stalks of wheat waving in the breeze. ("Your ears are like corn...", well, maybe not.)

In the next verse, he moves onto her teeth. Dental care was not available, so beautiful teeth would have been a rare occurrence. Hers are all still in place with none missing and are perfectly matched, as well as being as white as a row of washed and shorn sheep. Next he describes her mouth, followed by her temples, or in some translations, her cheeks, which remind him of pomegranates, probably for their color more than their shape.

Long slender necks were considered to be a form of beauty in this culture. The shields likely represent a necklace. There is no archaeological evidence of a tower of David existing. However, it may have been some sort of a watchtower. If this is the case, then the image could also be referring to the strength of his bride's character, which allows her to hold her head up high with confidence, or as someone who is very alert and vigilant.

Finally, the description of his bride ends with her breasts, which are likened to twin fawns grazing in the lilies. Lilies or lotus flowers were considered to be very beautiful and, within the culture, they were also representative of fertility. It has been suggested that the word picture may not be describing shape as much as the mood and intrigue that would draw a person's attention towards watching twin fawns grazing in a lotus field. Obviously, other interpretations are possible; let it suffice to say that he was visually pleased.

Verse 6 reminds us of poem 8 where the lover is invited to enjoy his bride's body for as long as the breeze of the day blows and the sun shines. This verse is basically a declaration by the groom that he is going to take his time to enjoy the experience of his honeymoon. In poem 5, the woman states that her lover is a sachet of myrrh resting between her breasts; now he is stating that he is going to the mountain of myrrh. There is probably no link between these poems, but the comment is a clear reference of his intentions towards her. In conclusion of this section, as he looks at his bride, he makes the declaration that he sees no physical flaws that would mire her beauty.

Finally, we arrive at verse 8 where the groom offers a clear invitation for his bride to go off with him as her husband. The place that she is leaving is both dangerous and uncertain, and is described as a lion's den and a mountain of leopards. However, the place where she is being invited to is safe because now she is with him. This ends the first half of this song, so I thought that it would be appropriate to interject a couple of marriage applications at this point. The second half of the poem likely takes place in the privacy of their room.

**Marriage Application (A):**

When we connect the first half of this poem with the theme of Love Redeemed, it tells men that it is okay to admire the beauty of their wives. After Adam and Eve sinned, the statement is made that they were no longer comfortable with their nakedness. God's redeeming love reinstates that comfort zone between husbands and wives. It is not wrong for a husband to enjoy his wife's body (even if she is shy about her appearance).

Wives, you may see flaws in your physical appearance, which keeps you from seeing your body as a beautiful gift to your husband. However, my guess is that he has a much greater appreciation and perspective on your body then you do. Wives, your bodies are a gift to your husbands, and Love Redeemed allows you to have the frame of mind, which tells you that it is okay to present yourselves to them with full confidence that your husband will admire and appreciate you. I once counseled a woman who had decided to not have sexual intimacy with her husband any longer because she had gained weight and did not want him to see her naked body. If you are a wife with this mind-set, then you owe it to your marriage to create a new perspective. A loving husband will delight in the experience of sexual intimacy with his wife regardless of her physical imperfections. Most husbands would be surprised with the list of imperfections that their wives see when they look in the mirror: these imperfections just don't even occur to them. Redeemed Love truly is blind.

Husbands, keep this in mind: wives are extremely sensitive when it comes to their appearance. To criticize or make fun of your wife's body should be considered by you to be one of the greatest errors you could ever make in your relationship. Quick off-the-cuff comments are not easily forgotten, even after many apologies. It is extremely important, husbands, that your wife knows that in your eyes she is a beautiful gift from God.

**Exercise:** Husbands, take the time to express to your wife how beautiful she is to you. Don't be afraid to be specific: she will love to hear what body parts appeal to you the most. Ask her how she feels about her own body. If she shares that she is not satisfied about some aspect of her physical appearance, take note but refrain from agreeing with her. Tell her instead that you believe that she is beautiful and that you love her as she is.

**Marriage Application (B):**

A second application comes from verse 8, where the bride is invited to go with the groom to a safe place. Love Redeemed requires that the husband creates a safe place for his wife. If the environment that you live in is not physically or emotionally safe for your wife and children, then it is time to change that environment. I once met with a couple that lived under the roof of someone else's home. It was obvious to me that the home environment was creating a wedge in their relationship. The home situation they were in created unexpected obligations to and from their hosts/landlords as well as emotional stress for both of them. My counsel was for them to find a new home as quickly as possible. If your home is not safe, then your relationship is sure to suffer. Husbands, sometimes your demeanor can also cause your home to not be a safe environment, either emotionally or physically. If you desire a healthy relationship, then you need to take immediate measures to correct the environment where your family lives.

**Exercise 2:** Discuss with your partner the safety of your home environment. This may include both physical and emotional security. If there are changes that can be made, then plan to take the necessary steps to make those alterations. If you are a partner with anger issues, then you should plan to find a counselor to help you deal with the emotional insecurity that you are creating in the home.

**Marriage Application (C):**

A third application comes in verse 9 where it is clear to see that he is deeply in love with his bride. Remaining crazy in love with your spouse requires work. Love Redeemed tells us that it is not an unrealistic expectation. It is, however, easy to get into routines where our marriages look more like a roommate agreement and where our attention to our spouse becomes divided. Consider what you are doing in your relationship to keep it alive and intimate.

**Exercise 3:** Spend some time reflecting on the routines of your married life. How are those routines impacting the intimacy of your relationship? Plan to shake up at least one of those routines that have placed your marriage into more of a roommate status, for the purpose of changing it into a vibrant, happy, married couple status.

**Allegorical Thought:**

The apostle Paul makes the following comment in Ephesians 5:27-28 "...so that he might present the church to himself in splendor, without spot or wrinkle or any such thing, that she might be holy and without blemish. In the same way husbands should love their wives..." This comment reminds me of our poem, as Paul paints a picture of the bride standing before Jesus, the groom, in purity and without any blemish. In the same way that the groom in this poem looks at his bride and describes her as beautiful, the church will someday stand before Jesus and hear the same words of endearment. As part of that body of believers, we each have a responsibility to prepare ourselves for that day.

**Exercise:** Imagine that you are standing before Jesus as His bride. As He looks at you and begins to describe you, He doesn't talk about your physical appearance, but about your spiritual heart condition. As He describes your thought life, what would He say? What would He say about your attitude, your compassion, and the way that you display the fruit of the Spirit (Galatians 5:22-23)? Would He be pleased with what He sees? If not, then it is time to begin a makeover by allowing the Spirit of God to make some transformations in your life. Choose the most troubling area that you need to modify, and then find a spiritual coach to help direct you through the process of change.

# Poem 11
# Part B - The Honeymoon
# 4:9-5:1

 

You have captivated my heart, my sister, my bride;
you have captivated my heart with one glance of your eyes,
with one jewel of your necklace.
<sup>10</sup> How beautiful is your love, my sister, my bride!
How much better is your love than wine,
and the fragrance of your oils than any spice!
<sup>11</sup> Your lips drip nectar, my bride;
honey and milk are under your tongue;
the fragrance of your garments is like the f
ragrance of Lebanon.
<sup>12</sup> A garden locked is my sister, my bride,
a spring locked, a fountain sealed.
<sup>13</sup> Your shoots are an orchard of pomegranates
with all choicest fruits,
henna with nard,
<sup>14</sup> nard and saffron, calamus and cinnamon,
with all trees of frankincense,
myrrh and aloes,
with all choice spices —
<sup>15</sup> a garden fountain, a well of living water,
and flowing streams from Lebanon.
<sup>16</sup> Awake, O north wind,
and come, O south wind!
Blow upon my garden,

let its spices flow.
Let my beloved come to his garden,
and eat its choicest fruits.
**5** I came to my garden, my sister, my bride,
I gathered my myrrh with my spice,
I ate my honeycomb with my honey,
I drank my wine with my milk.
Eat, friends, drink,
and be drunk with love!

We are now ready to move into the section of this poem that depicts the honeymoon couple as they encounter their first sexual intimacy. The wedding guests would still be celebrating, but it is now time for the couple to consummate their marriage by entering into their own private quarters. This would be a similar experience to what we have in traditional weddings today when the bride throws her bouquet and the groom her garter, and the couple waves good-bye and drives away for their honeymoon. The difference was that the couple did not have a way of booking a romantic holiday, so a tent was setup for the special occasion. The couple consummated their marriage in their private tent while the party continued.

In this second half of the poem, we begin with him sharing the same sentiments as the woman shares with him in the first poem. You may find it interesting to note that he uses the word "sister". This does not imply that he has married within his family, but that she is from his own clan, tribe or people group.

The song now moves from the visual to the aroma of her fragrance and a kiss, which is very sensual. It is interesting to note how the song uses the analogy of both milk and honey, which are also used to depict the Promised Land. Milk & Honey are words that the Old Testament uses symbolically to describe fertility and God's blessings on the land, which is very important to a culture that is dependent upon agriculture. A land flowing with milk implies an abundance of fertile cattle that have provided many calves, and a land flowing with honey infers much pollination, ensuring large crops, which are in bloom and will soon provide fruit. Her kiss therefore, implies the promise of much blessing.

The description of her garments would suggest at this point that she is still clothed. As the poem progresses, the bride is described as a locked garden, which very likely refers to her virginity. This is emphasized by the next line, which states that she is also a sealed fountain. The use of two metaphors to describe her virginity would indicate that great value was placed upon a bride entering her honeymoon bed as someone who had not been sexually active before marriage. It is important to note that he does not have access to this garden or fountain until she opens it up to him.

The next 2 verses describe the garden in much more detail. Her garden is a buffet of various plants, tastes and aromas. The idea is that there is much joy and pleasure to offer to all of his senses. Using the second metaphor of a water fountain, he notes that even though her fountain has been sealed until this day, there is clear indication that in this garden there is living water, not stagnant. Flowing water is also symbolic of life and is a requirement to sustain life.

It is at this point that the woman speaks for the first time in the poem. When she does, it is to give her new husband a welcome invitation to enter into her garden and to enjoy its fruits. It is important to note that she now calls her garden 'his' garden. We will also notice that, whereas in 2:7 & 3:5 there is a warning not to awaken love before the time is right, in this verse, after the marriage ceremony, we are told that it is now the time to wake up the winds. The winds from the North and South are called to stir up the fragrances in her garden, leaving us with an understanding that the winds of change are about to begin a new phase in this couple's relationship together, namely sexual intimacy. The groom, of course, accepts his bride's invitation, and enjoys with great delight everything that she offers to him. He has gathered. He has eaten. He has drunk. And for the time being, he is now fully satisfied.

The poem ends with the wedding guests voicing their approval, which would likely have been a common practice during the wedding celebration. Since the Song of Songs, as Scripture, is also the voice of God, in this poem, the final line should also be understood as God's voice to both of the lovers: "Eat, and drink your fill". In other words, you are married; so enjoy the passionate blessing of sexual intimacy (YES!).

**Marriage Application (A):**

It is important to pay attention to the fact that Love Redeemed recognizes the woman's right to protect her body. It also recognizes the value of entering into marriage as a virgin. Although in 1Corinthians 7:4 Paul states that in a marriage, our bodies belong sexually, to our spouse, it is still the woman's privilege to deny her body or to extend the invitation for her husband to explore her garden. This is not meant to be used as an opportunity for power and control, but it is meant to provide a mindset for the husband that speaks to the honor and privilege it is to be invited into his wife's garden. A husband should never take this invitation for granted, nor should he display an attitude of entitlement.

Love Redeemed also recognizes that the bride's body is to be a delight to her husband. It is therefore important for a wife to provide her husband with a garden that is inviting to his senses. This does not mean that she has to look like a model, but it does mean that it is important for her garden to be maintained. Sometimes, when life gets busy, it's easy to drop the extra care required for a wife to maintain her body. However, wives, it is important to keep your husband attracted to your garden so that he doesn't lose interest or is tempted to explore a garden that is not rightly his to explore. If he seems uninterested in you sexually, one area to examine is how well your garden has been maintained. I would encourage you to be aware of what he adores in you physically, and then make sure that he is often enticed by the garden you offer to him.

**Exercise 1:** This exercise is for the wives. If you haven't taken the time to care for yourself lately, then I would suggest that you do something this week to enhance your garden. Not only will this be a delight to him, but it will also be uplifting to you. So, treat yourself to a makeover in at least one area of your physical beauty. On the other hand, if you are doing well in this department, simply make a special effort to offer a new delight to his senses the next time you make love.

**Marriage Application (B):**

God's plan for Love Redeemed also allows for unrestrained, liberal enjoyment within the context of the marriage bed. If you are placing too many boundaries and taboos on your times of sexual intimacy, then you need to consider if God desires to free you of some of your restraints. A clear boundary to remember is that this is not a public garden for everyone. It is restricted to you and your spouse. This clearly means that third parties are not allowed to enter, even in picture and movie form.

Another way that the marriage bed can have too many people in it is through the echoing voice of your parents, and possibly even the church, if they have convinced you that sex is not to be enjoyed or that certain sexual activities are not allowed. Feel free to turn on the lights and the music. Remove the covers and the inhibitions that the Bible does not directly speak out against. If it is not painful to your partner or offensive, then allow Love Redeemed to unlock the gates that your parents and well-meaning Christians have barred during your singleness. God approves of great sexual intimacy. He wants both the husband and the wife to be fully satisfied with pleasure and gratitude. Love Redeemed provides the freedom to enjoy God's creation of pleasure as it is experienced by all of your senses through sexual intimacy.

**Allegorical Thought:**

Revelation 19:7-9; 21:2-4,9-11 all refer to the day when the groom, who is Christ, will come for his bride, and they will enjoy the garden of heaven together. Most of us would have difficulty bringing our minds to the point of considering a honeymoon with God. However, the aspects of sexual intimacy that provide unashamed transparency, closeness and purity, as well as feelings of fulfillment and joy, will all be part of the experience of heaven and, for the most part, should also be a part of sexual intimacy with our marriage partner.

Shannon Ethridge in her book, The Passion Principles, talks about the day when her professor asked her class the question, "How is your relationship with God sexual in nature?" The class was initially taken back by the question but, upon further consideration, was able to come up with a list of about twenty-two different ways.

Some of these included such things as: trust, pleasure, vulnerability, humility and communion. [9]

**Exercise:** Consider the emotional purity of your sexual experience. What are the pleasures that you experience? Since God is the creator of our pleasurable feelings, senses and sexual intimacy, consider the joy of your sexual experience as a gift from God. It is highly likely that these pleasurable experiences are a foreshadowing of what is in store for the believer in heaven. Reflect on this and give praise to Jesus, the groom of the church, his bride.

---

[9] Shannon Ethridge, *The Passion Principles* (Nashville: Thomas Nelson, 2014) pp.7-8.

# POEM 12
## PART A – THE PURSUIT
## 5:2-8

I slept, but my heart was awake.
A sound! My beloved is knocking.
"Open to me, my sister, my love,
my dove, my perfect one,
for my head is wet with dew,
my locks with the drops of the night."
³ I had put off my garment;
how could I put it on?
I had bathed my feet;
how could I soil them?
⁴ My beloved put his hand to the latch,
and my heart was thrilled within me.
⁵ I arose to open to my beloved,
and my hands dripped with myrrh,
my fingers with liquid myrrh,
on the handles of the bolt.
⁶ I opened to my beloved,
but my beloved had turned and gone.
My soul failed me when he spoke.
I sought him, but found him not;
I called him, but he gave no answer.
⁷ The watchmen found me
as they went about in the city;
they beat me, they bruised me,

they took away my veil,
those watchmen of the walls.
[8] I adjure you, O daughters of Jerusalem,
if you find my beloved,
that you tell him
I am sick with love.

On first reading, it is somewhat difficult to understand this poem, as it has the tendency to read from a narrative perspective. Some people even understand this poem or song to be a description of a dream that she is having. However, I believe that it would be better to understand this poem as the expression of powerful and yet difficult emotions in the face of marital struggles, for the purpose of teaching us how Love Redeemed helps couples deal with discord in their relationships. Once again, because of the length of this poem I have divided it into 2 parts.

Culturally speaking, for the time that it was written, the poem is extremely radical. For a woman to be out in the streets at night searching for her husband would be unheard of and would, in fact, be considered a shameful practice. This counter-cultural approach is common in the Song of Songs and is not unlike some of Jesus' parables. A great example of this is the parable of the prodigal son, in which the youngest son offends his father to the extreme by demanding his inheritance before his father's death. The son receives his inheritance and goes off to a foreign land where he wastes everything. Eventually, the son returns to the father, and the parable becomes even more counter-cultural when the father responds with unabashed love in the way he accepts his son's return back into the family as if no offence had occurred. In the same way, this woman unashamedly pursues her lost love in a day when this would have been totally unacceptable. Both the parable of the prodigal son and this song show us that the power of love is sometimes required to supersede culture and offence for the sake of restoring a relationship.

The counter-cultural risk that the woman takes in this poem is reinforced by the way the watchmen of the city treat her for pursuing her husband through the streets at night. However, since the poem is seeking to demonstrate the power of love, it is necessary for the woman to do the pursuing. Had the poet written this poem with the husband doing the pursuing, the message on the power of love would have been significantly reduced. At the time when this poem was written, a man's wife was considered to be his property, so it would have been only natural for him to pursue her. His motives for seeking out his lost wife could, in fact, be many, some maybe not too pure; however, all motives would have been culturally acceptable. Her motive, on the other hand, to take such a risk, could only be driven by love. Therefore, in order to advance the theme of Love Redeemed, the author has wisely chosen to make this poem radically counter-cultural in an attempt to show us the strength of love in working through relationship difficulties.

This poem is not just about what appears to be a wife's teasing gone wrong because her husband completely misinterprets the tease, but as already mentioned, also describes the impact of love, which allows the couple to overcome their predicament. This song describes a couple that struggles with misreading each other's communication signals. Most couples that have been married for any length of time are able to resonate with this experience (no new insights here). Miscommunication is one of the easiest mistakes we make, and is often a source of conflict between couples. Love Redeemed provides grace within a marriage, and as we will see, also provides persistence to correct whatever wrongs may have been committed towards one another.

## LOVE REDEEMED

Some commentators see the entire song to be layered with sexual innuendos that would have been clearly understood at the time of writing, thereby making the poem to be extremely erotic. Personally, I think they have gone too far with this focus, since it significantly distracts the reader from seeing other possible interpretations that are less erotic and that actually provide a message with regards to the redemption and power of love. Another reason not to focus on the euphemisms that may or may not have been erotic images is that most of these are now lost in our generation and culture. I think that it is too shallow to accept that this passage of Scripture is given to us for the sole purpose of allowing couples permission to enjoy fully liberated sexual intimacy. That interpretation seems to lose the significance of her pursuit.

In this song, the woman is excited to hear her lover's voice on the other side of the door, but for reasons she describes as practical inconveniences, she is somewhat reluctant to get out of her bed and open the door. Since her actions do not coincide with her heart's desire or her thoughts, my guess is that she is either flirting with or teasing him, or simply being lazy. Unfortunately, he doesn't catch on to this as a tease and so he is totally confused. (What man hasn't found himself in this predicament?) Eventually, he comes to the wrong conclusion; he believes that he is being rejected, so he leaves.

It is possible that women readers will understand this song better than my male readers. Instead of understanding her comments to be a tease, the poem may be describing the emotional wrestling that the woman is going through by not initially being in the mood for her lover's invitation, but yet, at the same time, she desires to be with her lover. Ironically, at the beginning of the song she says that she doesn't have the motivation to let him into her bed. After all, she would have to soil her feet and put her robe back on. However, when she discovers her lackadaisical or coy attitude has caused him to leave, she quickly finds the motivation and energy to get out of bed and pursue him.

The remainder of the poem describes her pursuit and the challenges she is faced with as she searches for her lost love. We shouldn't be too quick to assume that by the end of the song, the lover has been found in his garden and that he is now grazing among the lilies, which is a euphemism for making love to his wife. Instead we might be better to interpret the last two verses as her saying to the women, "Our marriage has been properly consummated; he belongs to me, so back off if you have any ideas of stealing him from me."

Since this is a somewhat difficult poem to grasp, I believe that it would be beneficial at this point to go back to its beginning and attempt a more detailed examination of the song. The song begins with the woman being awakened by a knock on her door by her husband. Apparently, she was not sleeping very soundly, as she suggests that her heart was awake. He wants to enter, and so he tells her that his head is wet with dew. This may suggest that, as a shepherd, he was sleeping under the stars. We are actually not told why they are separated from each other; they may have had an argument, or he has come home later than she thinks he should be out. The "why" is ambiguous, which allows for us to fill in the blanks, and opens the poem to a broad range of applications that we can apply to our own lives in answer to the question, "Why might I, at times, block the way for my partner to be close to me?"

An important item to note is that he seeks to compel her to open the door by using terms of endearment. Clearly, whatever the cause is for the door to have been locked, he is making an attempt to break down the barriers. She, however, as already discussed, is reluctant to open the door. The question that is raised is, why? Is she teasing him? Or, is she upset with him for being late coming home? Or, is there another reason that we are not being told? Whatever the case, she tells him that she has taken off her clothes and doesn't want to put them back on again. She has also washed her feet and doesn't want to soil them on the way to the door. Both of these are fairly lame excuses, which may be reflective of petty disagreements, or, as we have already suggested, may also have been meant to be a simple way of playing 'hard to get'. The teasing idea may be reinforced in verse 4 where we read that her heart is thrilled with the idea of him breaking in, and also when later she is so quick to pursue him. It seems that her intention all along is to let him in, but that for the moment she is choosing to lead him on. Whatever her motive may be, she is playing a game with his emotions that unfortunately, she will soon discover, has its dangers.

His impatience causes him to attempt to break into the room, and she is thrilled by his pursuit. Unfortunately, the door remains shut to him. Like the garden gate in the previous poem, they both discover that she must do the opening to invite him in. It is probably fair to say that the process of what is happening took more time to play out than it appears, because by the time she reaches the door to open it, he has given up and has disappeared. If we understand this part of the poem in a literal sense, (rather than the erotic sense mentioned above) her hands were not likely dripping with myrrh while she was lying in bed. Therefore, we can assume that, before coming to open the door, she has taken the time to anoint or prepare herself. Likely, her intentions are to make sure that she presents herself to him in the best and most desirable way possible. Unfortunately, by the time she arrives, he has given up his pursuit and has left. We are therefore led to believe that he interpreted her playfulness as a major rejection. Alas, we are privy to a relationship breakdown, which has been caused by that age-old challenge of couples not clearly communicating with one another.

**Marriage Application (A):**

Once again, because this poem is so long, I have chosen to intersperse marriage applications among my interpretations of the poem. Our first marriage application, (you guessed it) is on communication.

Couples who have been successfully married for many years seem to instinctively know, because of past experiences, how their partner will respond to a variety of situations, whereas newlyweds have much to learn in this department. This poem is a clear example of a communication failure, since what she was saying to him did not correspond with what she was feeling for him. Men are often not very good at discerning this kind of discrepancy. When a woman says "no", it may take us a while to realize that what she may really be saying is "convince me". Therefore, especially early in a marriage, one of the things that couples need to do a lot more of is to over-communicate. What I mean by this is to make sure that you are communicating in such a way that you are not relying on the other person to assume any part of your message. For example, "I will meet you at 4pm."

assumes that the other person knows where you will meet. In the case of this poem, had the woman said to her husband who was standing outside of the door, "I will unlatch the door in a minute; just give me time to prepare myself," it very likely would have kept him from leaving, and the remainder of the evening would have been very different.

**Exercise:** Try practicing over-communication this week, to see if the results benefit your relationship. Think about what you are communicating, and then ask yourself if there are any assumptions that could be misinterpreted. This kind of communication is also very transparent; there are no guesses as to what is happening on the other side of the door. It is not disrespectful, if said with a concerned and loving tone, to ask the other person to confirm what you have just communicated so that you know the message has come through clearly.

**Back to verse 6:**

When the woman discovers that her lover has disappeared, she is most distressed. The NIV and the NLT (New Living Translation) do not quite capture the meaning of the line in verse 6, which actually reads "my soul failed me when he spoke." The Hebrew definition of the word that has been translated 'soul' in this verse is the word used to describe our natural inclinations, or what is commonly known in Christian circles as the desires of the flesh. It is the voice of temptation that encourages greed, lust, anger, etc. It is also the voice that lacks self-discipline. It is the whisper that gives you permission to eat that piece of chocolate cake, when you are in the middle of a weight-loss program. It is the permission that you give yourself to keep on sinning when your conscience tells you "No!" This is the voice that she was listening to, when she refused to open the door. However, now she realizes that this voice, as it so often does, has failed her; as a result, she has lost her lover. In other words, she realizes that her response to his request was the wrong response. She had listened to the wrong voice.

**Marriage Application (B):**

It is important to be careful regarding which voice you are listening to, especially in terms of your spouse. If you listen to the wrong voice, it will put distance between you and your partner. Constantly check your assumptions before believing they are truth. Beware, especially, of the blame game. Learn to guard your heart against improper thoughts, especially negative ones.

In Philippians 4:7-8, Paul teaches us how to protect our hearts. The key that Paul gives in this passage is connected to our prayer life. Not long ago, I was significantly disappointed by a message my friend gave me. Before I knew what was happening, I was listening to the wrong voice and was beginning to feel resentment towards the messenger, which was impacting my decision to accept an invitation to spend time with him. I had to turn to Philippians to remind myself how to guard my heart.

There are four steps to the Philippians 4:7-8 process, which are all done in an attitude of prayer, asking God to speak truth into the situation.

**Step 1:** Attempt to shift your perspective so that you try to see the situation from the other person's viewpoint. Sometimes we call this empathizing, at other times it is simply a matter of understanding.

**Step 2:** Look for opportunities of gratitude within the situation. What are the things that we can give praise to God for?
**Step 3:** Check your motives. Are your motives pure, or are you deceiving yourself?
**Step 4:** Hand the situation over to God. Make the problem His and not yours.

If you follow these four steps, Philippians tells you that you will experience peace that goes beyond your own understanding.

**Exercise:** If you are dealing with resentment towards your partner over some failed expectations or disappointments, then I would encourage you to take the time to work through the four steps of the Philippians process. Do not allow yourself to brood over negative thoughts.

**Back to verse 7:**

This is a strange verse, in that the woman doesn't seem to be set back very much, (if at all) in her pursuit of her lover, even though she is beaten and socially shamed. This is one of the reasons many see this entire song as a dream.

The inference in this verse is that her nakedness has been exposed to the watchmen. In the ESV, it is her veil that is removed, but in the NIV, it is her cloak that is removed. The actual word, which is translated "took away", is more typically used to describe the spreading out of a cloth, such as putting a tablecloth on a table or a blanket on the ground. The idea is that her covering has been opened up to the public, so that she is no longer hidden. Like a tablecloth, she has been spread out for all to see. If she was using a veil to mask her face, the watchmen have intentionally removed it to expose her face. She has, therefore, suffered great shame at the hands of the watchmen.

The watchmen are men with authority who have the power to assist but who have no interest in her predicament; in fact they use her predicament to punish her. Those from whom she might have had expectations for assistance in helping her to find her lover have actually taken advantage of her situation by abusing her and removing her veil. Culturally, they have shamed her by implying that she is a loose woman. Keep in mind that in this culture, it was not acceptable for a woman to go about pursuing a man (only prostitutes did this). We were introduced to this cultural concept in chapter 2:7, where she makes the comment "Why should I be like one who veils herself?" The irony of this situation is that now, not only are her feet soiled, which would have been a small price to pay for opening the door, but now her whole reputation has been soiled. By not attending to an easier problem, that of opening the door to her husband, she now has a much more difficult situation to resolve. In order to sustain a healthy marriage, there is always the work of making sure that things, which need to be resolved, don't get ignored for lack of motivation.

The beating she received was not so severe that she could not continue her search. What is important to note is that the context speaks to the commitment of her love. Her love commitment requires her to be placed into the dangers of the street and of going against what is socially acceptable, as well as the punishment enforced by the authorities. Love Redeemed clearly points out that reconciliation requires, at times, a love that is more powerful than social boundaries and prejudices.

Since she has not had success with the watchmen, she now turns to the daughters of Jerusalem. There seems to be a time gap between her search through the streets at night and the time when she runs into the daughters of Jerusalem. It is highly unlikely, because of the watchmen, that the daughters of Jerusalem would have been out at night, so it seems that she is now continuing her search during the day. Her message to the daughters of Jerusalem is that she is sick with love. In other words, she is no longer listening to a voice that makes her ambivalent as to the state of her heart's interest, but she is now keenly aware of how deeply she misses her husband and lover. In fact, it is so important that her lover receives the right message, that she now asks the women to place themselves under oath to give him the message that she is faint, weak and sick with love. Her message may be an exaggeration of her feelings, but the purpose is to end all questions in her lover's mind. She is interested in him, and she will definitely open the door to receive him back into her life.

The daughters of Jerusalem respond with the question, "What makes him so special, that you call upon us for assistance, and make us provide you with such a promise?" It seems that this group of women wants to know what's in it for them. They may also be wondering, "If he is so great, why has she allowed him to leave her?" Note, in 6:1, that these women do not pledge to give him the message of her love, but instead ask her to point them in the right direction so that they can find this man. I believe that the inference is that the relationship is vulnerable and that they would like an opportunity to cash in on this vulnerable situation and to have him for themselves. Therefore, her response to them is that he belongs to her; "he can be found grazing in 'his garden,'" is her reply. In other words, "Leave him alone; he already has a meadow, and I am it." Notice how she ends this dialogue in vs. 3 "I am my lover's and my lover is mine..."

**Marriage Enrichment (C):**

It is important, ladies, to stake your territory. There will always be predators who are interested in claiming what is yours, especially if they sense that there is a weakness in the relationship waiting to be breached. What are you proactively doing to make sure that your man is not inclined to be prey to other women? The following are five suggestions that may help:
1. Make sure that you affirm him often. We are all drawn to someone who affirms us and whose actions show that they believe in us. These are the people we crave to be with, and they are also the people we don't want to let down. If you are not affirming, then you have left the door open for someone else to capture his heart.
2. Spend time together. If he is not lonely, then he is less likely to be seeking companionship elsewhere.
3. Practice transparency. Couples that hide information from each other are setting themselves up for trust issues and suspicion, which open the door to a voice of justification such as, "She doesn't trust me anyway so I might as well be unfaithful."
4. Keep flirting with him. Men love to feel that they are attractive to women. Make sure that he knows that he doesn't have to look outside of his home

for a woman who is attracted to him. Along with this, keep him sexually fulfilled.
5. Pay attention to your physical appearance. It is important that you don't become lazy in this department. When he married you, he was attracted to you in many ways. (You can be pretty sure that one of those attractions was the physical you.) Age, hard work and children can have their toll on physical attractiveness, which most husbands understand. However, they still expect you to make an effort to present yourself regularly in a way that appeals to their eyes.

**Exercise:** Examine your relationship. If you are falling short in any of the above, I would encourage you to work on protecting your marriage.

**Allegorical Thought:**

The first thing that jumps to my mind with regards to this poem is Revelation 3:20, where Jesus says to the church of Laodicea "Behold I stand at the door and knock. If anyone hears my voice and opens the door, I will come in to him and eat with him, and he with me." It is interesting that the church of Laodicea is being chastised for their indifference in their relationship with Christ. They are neither hot nor cold. The Revelation passage talks about how they are too comfortable in their self-sufficiency, which is not unlike the woman in this poem who is comfortably in her bed, and ready to retire for the night. Jesus' plea to the Laodicean church is to be allowed to bless them with pure riches, white garments, healing and fellowship. In other words, Jesus' message is to stop being so self-sufficiently independent that you have no room for the intimate relationship that He desires to offer to you.

At this time in your life, God may be persistently knocking to get your attention. However, if you delay, you may miss out on the blessing that he is seeking to offer to you. He desires to change your present situation. At present, you may be accepting gold or financial blessings that are less than purified. Or, the nakedness of shame rather than the garments of righteousness that he offers. Or, the blindness of your circumstances when he wants to offer you sight. Maybe you are settling for spiritual loneliness when, if you were to open the door, you would discover that Jesus desires to be your guest.

**Exercise:** Are there areas in your life where the doors are closed to Christ's fellowship because of your indifference to God's call for you to make changes? If this is the case, the challenge is to confess and then open your arms to gift of the relationship that he desires to offer to you instead of the inferior alternative that you are currently content with. This is a good time to practice the prayer of *'examen'*. Before God, allow a time of quietness where you invite Jesus to come into your spiritual home and clean house.

# Poem 12
## Part B – The Pursuit
## 5:9-6:3

⁹ What is your beloved more than another beloved,
O most beautiful among women?
What is your beloved more than another beloved,
that you thus adjure us?
¹⁰ My beloved is radiant and ruddy,
distinguished among ten thousand.
¹¹ His head is the finest gold;
his locks are wavy,`
black as a raven.
¹² His eyes are like doves
beside streams of water,
bathed in milk,
sitting beside a full pool.
¹³ His cheeks are like beds of spices,
mounds of sweet-smelling herbs.
His lips are lilies,
dripping liquid myrrh.
¹⁴ His arms are rods of gold,
set with jewels.
His body is polished ivory,
bedecked with sapphires.
¹⁵ His legs are alabaster columns,
set on bases of gold.
His appearance is like Lebanon,

choice as the cedars.
¹⁶ His mouth is most sweet,
and he is altogether desirable.
This is my beloved and this is my friend,
O daughters of Jerusalem.
⁶ Where has your beloved gone,
O most beautiful among women?
Where has your beloved turned,
that we may seek him with you?
² My beloved has gone down to his garden
to the beds of spices,
to graze in the gardens
and to gather lilies.
³ I am my beloved's and my beloved is mine;
he grazes among the lilies.

From verse 9 to 16 we are given a description of the husband. It is somewhat strange that the wife does not describe the character qualities of her lover, but instead, she only describes his physical attributes. Maybe the simple reason for this is that only a physical description is required in order for the daughters of Jerusalem to find him among the other men. There may also be euphemisms and metaphors that she uses which we understand only as physical descriptions, but in her culture had a much deeper meaning.

She begins with a description of his skin, which is radiant, a word usually suggestive of health and happiness. He is also ruddy (red), which generally describes someone who has spent time outside. This would be typical of a shepherd, and is used to describe David's complexion at the time when he was anointed king (1 Samuel 16:12). It is highly unlikely from this description that she is describing King Solomon.

Verse 11 describes his head, which she says is pure gold. In the Middle East, the head is the place of highest honor, whereas the feet are the place of lowest honor and are considered to be a source of shame. Gold is a precious metal and generally speaks of great wealth, value and honor. By suggesting that his head is gold, she is inferring upon him her greatest respect.

It seems that, to my North American mindset, she does a better job of describing his hair than the man does in the previous poem. She simply states that it is black like the color of a raven, and wavy, which is pretty much how he describes her hair, but instead he uses the metaphor of a flock of sheep descending from a mountain. Like her, his eyes are also like doves, but his are drinking from a stream. The doves have been washed in milk so they are white. In the NIV, they are mounted like jewels, but in the ESV they are beside a full pool of water. The inference in our language would probably be that he has large, beautiful, dreamy eyes.

His cheeks are like beds of spices, or mounds of sweet-smelling herbs. She seems to be describing his aroma more than a visual picture of his cheeks. His lips are lilies dripping with myrrh. Myrrh in the Song of Songs often relates to a state of being sexually aroused. I am guessing that she is suggesting that his lips entice her to want to kiss them. Earlier, her hands were dripping with myrrh; now his lips are dripping with myrrh.

Verse 14 moves us from his head to a description of his arms. Once again, she attributes to them the value of gold in the same way that she has spoken of his head. She then describes his body as being ivory. Tremper Longman III suggests that this is a euphemism for a part of the male anatomy that reminds her of an ivory tusk.[10] However, if she is giving a physical description of him to these women so that they can help find him, then it wouldn't make sense that she would be drawing their attention to his genitals. I think that we can more likely assume that she is describing his chest and abdomen. Finally, we move to a description of his legs and stature. Once again, gold is referenced as well as marble. The trees of Lebanon were considered to be very majestic and beautiful, and their wood was highly prized. It is quite likely that she is suggesting that he is tall with strong legs. We should notice that the feet are not described, since it is an embarrassment in this culture to draw attention to the feet. She ends her description with

---

[10] Tremper Longman III, *The New International Commentary on the Old Testament – Song of Songs* (Grand Rapids: Eerdmans, 2001) p.173.

a comment regarding her desire to give him a big, juicy kiss. Probably, her description of him has reminded her of how much she misses him and how much sexual appeal his body has for her.

The remaining verses, from verse 17 to the end of the poem, are, in my opinion, a statement to the daughters of Jerusalem that the man they are looking for is already vowed to her by marriage. He is not available to them because he already has a pasture to graze in, which is her. So ladies, "hands off"! If you accept this interpretation, then the poem ends without her finding him, and the reader is left to wonder about the ending. The reality is that not all pursuits end well. Therefore, we must be prudent in how we speak and treat one another, as offences are not always easy to reconcile.

**Marriage Application:**

At first glance, a marriage application for this section may not be obvious. The first question we might want to ask is, "Wives, what is your impression of your husband? Do you see the gold in his mind, arms and legs, which represent his thoughts, strength, protection and stability?" The second question may be: "Men, how do you strive to measure up? Is your character something your wife can easily describe as gold? Are you honoring her by taking care of your body?" Luckily for most of us, Love Redeemed allows us to see positive qualities in our spouses. If when you look at your spouse, your mind goes into negative mode and you can see only those things that you wish were different, then it is time to refocus and to work on a new perspective.

If we are like most people, our minds are often drawn to thoughts related to our physical appearance and how attractive we are, especially to our spouse. Wives, the bottom line is that he does want you to be attracted to him. Some husbands may be overly obsessed with keeping in shape, while other husbands show little or no interest. In a healthy relationship, balance is important. Eating properly and exercising sufficiently in order to maintain healthy bodies is a gift that both partners can give to each other. There are so many relationship benefits when both parties feel physically fit and confident in how they appear to one another.

**Exercise:** Take the time to evaluate what you are doing to be as healthy as possible within your current circumstances. What adjustments do you need to make? As a gift to yourself and to your partner, make one positive life-style change this week to move you closer to being a more physically fit person.

**Summary thoughts:**

I have already mentioned several possible marriage applications throughout our discussion of the poem, but in summary it is important to comment that Love Redeemed recognizes that we are human, and that marriage partners will not always be on the same page when it comes to communication, including the expression of our sexual desires. When difficulties in these areas arise, they cannot be left unattended. When one partner is in flight mode, then the other partner needs to be in pursuit (or fight) mode.

This song also seems to address the danger of taking your marriage partner for granted. In this scenario, the woman assumes that her lover will be at the door when she finally decides to open it, but then she discovers that he is no longer pursuing. He also has made the assumption that she will beckon to his call and quickly open the door at any hour. One of the challenges within many marriages is that most men do not handle rejection well.

Another possible way of interpreting this poem is to see it as a song that speaks of responsibility within the marriage. In a subtle way, this poem may suggest that the woman, by failing to open the door at her lover's request is responsible for his leaving. In recognizing this she also sees it is as her responsibility to become pro-active by seeking to find him in order to resolve the dilemma. This reminds me of Matthew 18:15 where God has given us the responsibility of reconciliation, when we know there is a problem.

Except for the radical counter-cultural shock value that I mentioned earlier, I'm not sure why it is, that in both poems 10 and 12, it is the woman who is pursuing her husband. However, maybe this is a reflection of the continued struggle women have with the curse of Genesis 3 where she is told that she will pursue after her husband? In Love Redeemed, the curse continues to be in effect like a contagious disease, but a solution or remedy is now available to counter the negative impact and to begin healing.

Finally, the poem also points out that when we rely on others to assist us, it may come with some dangers. Two examples are given in the song, where first she has to deal with a group of men who see her failings as offensive, vulnerable and worthy of retribution, and then secondly, we have a group of women who see her failings as an opportunity. When we make mistakes, there is always a cost that comes with reconciliation; often that cost is at the expense of our pride. There is also a time when the relationship is vulnerable. Therefore, it is important to not allow the relationship to continue with unresolved issues, but to resolve them as quickly as possible.

**Allegorical Thought:**

In this section of the poem, the lover is described as a very physically handsome and desirable lover. Within Christian circles we tend to describe and want to envision Jesus as beautiful and desirable. However, Isaiah makes the following comments about Jesus: "He was despised and rejected by men; a man of sorrows, and acquainted with grief; and as one from whom men hide their faces he was despised, and we esteemed him not." (Isaiah 53:3). It is not the physical character of Jesus that makes Him attractive. Jesus was God manifested (visualized) in the flesh (a human body), yet when God chose to reveal Himself to us in the flesh, he did not choose to be the most physically attractive person on earth. Those of us who think their physical appearance does not measure up, can obtain great comfort and encouragement from this knowledge. However, this does not mean that our character should be equally flawed. Here is where we have the responsibility to be like Jesus. As God in the flesh, Jesus revealed the remarkable character of God in every way.

**Exercise:** Take some time to look in the mirror and to praise God that He looks on the inward character of a person and not on the outside. Thank Him that Jesus was not the most physically attractive person in the world, which allows you, as you look at your physical imperfections, to identify with Jesus. Remind yourself that it is more important for you to work on the character of your life than on the outward attraction of your body. How would you compare the time you spend on your outward appearance to the time you spend on your character beauty?

# Poem 13
## Surpassing Beauty
## 6:4-10

~

You are beautiful as Tirzah, my love,
lovely as Jerusalem,
awesome as an army with banners.
⁵ Turn away your eyes from me,
for they overwhelm me—
Your hair is like a flock of goats
leaping down the slopes of Gilead.
⁶ Your teeth are like a flock of ewes
that have come up from the washing;
all of them bear twins;
not one among them has lost its young.
⁷ Your cheeks are like halves of a pomegranate
behind your veil.
⁸ There are sixty queens and eighty concubines,
and virgins without number.
⁹ My dove, my perfect one, is the only one,
the only one of her mother,
pure to her who bore her.
The young women saw her and called her blessed;
the queens and concubines also, and they praised her.
¹⁰ "Who is this who looks down like the dawn,
beautiful as the moon, bright as the sun,
awesome as an army with banners?"

This poem or song has what is known as an *'inclusio'*, which makes it easy to distinguish as a separate poem from the previous and following verses. The *'inclusio'* in this poem is the phrase "awesome (majestic) as an army with banners" Like literary bookends the poem begins and ends with the same phrase. The NIV for some reason, changes the last line to "as majestic as the stars in procession." Unfortunately, this hides the *'inclusio'*. Since the NIV does not take into account the *'inclusio'* in this poem, it interprets the following poem as a continuation of this poem. By doing this it makes what I believe to be a mistake in the following poem by attributing the speaking voice to the man instead of the woman. As you will see when we get to poem 14, to attribute the voice to the man significantly altars the interpretation.

With that being said, let us get back to the poem or song at hand. This song clearly begins with the man describing his lovely woman as majestic or as awesome as an army with banners. It ends with a group of women proclaiming the same message. This literary style of a group of women affirming the opening comments gives weight or validity to his comment, especially since the group of women are queens and concubines of great beauty. To have the queens and concubines make this statement would be like the most gorgeous women in the world gathering together to proclaim that his woman is the most beautiful of them all. The fact that we are using queens and concubines as well as armies in this poem would indicate that this is not likely a shepherd speaking, but that this poem could easily be one of Solomon's works.

You may find it interesting that the speaker uses a military term to describe the beauty of a woman, but if the words are those of a king, an army, to him, could very will be seen as beautiful, as it would be a significant comfort to see his armed forces gathered on a mountain as a show of force and loyalty.

The dictionary of Biblical Imagery points out that "Banners are identifying flags or streamers attached to the end of a standard. Throughout history they have served three main purposes: a) to identify a group, b) to claim possession of a space or territory and c) to lend festivity to a celebration."[11] All three of the purposes above would give importance to the woman that he is describing. Her beauty gives him identity by making a statement about his ability to capture the attention of such a desirable woman. Her beauty also reminds him that she is his by commitment, which gives him cause for great joy and celebration. Therefore, in this poem, her banner is beauty, whereas the woman in poem 7 (2:4) describes the banner over her man to be love. In that poem, love is the identifying behavior that describes his relationship to her. In this poem, her beauty is the banner or standard that captures the attention of all who see her, and seems to be the identifying feature of this relationship.

Two cities are described in this poem. The first city is Tirzah. The name Tirzah means "She is my delight". Tirzah replaced Shechem, as the second capital city of the Northern Kingdom, and was later replaced by Samaria. This may provide us with a reference to the time of the writing of this poem; however, if this is the case, then it is of interest to note that the poem was written long

---

[11] I have added the alpha bullets to provide greater clarity between the 3 purposes. *The Dictionary of Biblical Imagery,* General ed. Leland Ryken, James C. Wilhoit, Tremper Longman III (Downers Grove: Inter Varsity Press, 1998) p.70.

after the time of King Solomon. Jerusalem means "rain of peace", suggesting the blessing of God in providing a soft rain for the crops. Interestingly, Jerusalem was the capital of the South, so we have both the capital cities of Israel and of Judah used to describe the woman. The two meanings together would state that, "She is a delight and a blessing of God". There may be a double meaning being used here where the man is comparing her to both the actual meanings of the city names, and the importance of the cities. These two cities were actually enemies of each other, so he is portraying the woman he loves as two cities that were in conflict with each other. However, the fact that the military banners are mentioned may suggest that there is a truce between the two countries, which is being upheld by the presence of the two armies. This leaves me wondering if her beauty also has something to do with her disposition of exhibiting peace while being under tension.

As we move onto the next verse, he beckons her to turn her eyes away from him, because they unsettle him. Like the banners and the cities, which represent glory and power, her eyes are overwhelming in their beauty. Her eyes may also represent a power that she has over him, as well as being her glory. The rest of the description of her is similar to that of 4:1-2 from poem 12.

After describing her in some detail, he then begins to compare her to all other women. First, she is compared to queens who have a royal position and access to all of the resources necessary to make them beautiful. However, even with all of these resources at hand, none of the sixty queens are able to measure up to her. Secondly, she is compared to the concubines. A concubine is a slave, whose main purpose is to provide sexual pleasure to her master. There is no marriage commitment in a concubine relationship, but the master is expected to care for and protect his concubine as if she were a wife. Children from a concubine would be cared for, but they would not receive an inheritance or title. In later years the role of the concubine was taken over by the role of a mistress. Knowing the role and purposes of a concubine, gives more significance to the comment that none of them are able to compete with the woman that is being described in this poem who is more physically beautiful than all of the queens, and as a lover, she is also able to outshine all of the concubines.

The woman is compared to a third group of women: this is the group of young, unmarried and eligible women who are too innumerable to be counted. The innocence and purity of a virgin has always been prized throughout generations and in most cultures. Using literary license that allows for exaggeration, our lover portrays his wife as having even more value to him than all of the virgins he could summon. He has now bestowed upon her three great attributes. She is more beautiful and majestic than sixty queens, she is a more sexually adequate lover than eighty concubines, and her innocence and purity is more attractive than all virgins, much more than can be numbered.

Finally, we discover that, not only does she rise above the three categories of desirable women mentioned above, but she is also highly valued among her own family members. She is so unique that, even among her siblings, there is no one else like her. In fact, she is the most cherished and loved child out of all of her mother's children (sounds a bit like Joseph the son of Jacob). Of course, all of this praise that is lavished upon her seems to be exaggerated to poetically raise her up as the most gorgeous and attractive woman of all women.

However, with all that has been said, he sees it is as still not adequate to describe his attractive wife. Therefore, in order to emphasize even more how amazingly perfect and gorgeous she is, he ends his poem with the queens and concubines also praising her. As a result, the poem ends with the endearing soliloquy of both the queens and the concubines who look at her and wonder, "Who is this person who is even capable of out-shining the sun and the moon?"

**Marriage Application:**

There are two applications that I would like to suggest for this poem. Let's begin with the easy one. Men, what value are you bestowing upon your wife? In the same way that the poet praises his wife, when you look at your wife, it is important for you to share sentiments that reflect your appreciation of her beauty. If you are not already in the habit of making your wife feel like the most beautiful woman that God has created under the moon and the stars that has ever crossed your path, then now is the time to begin. The wife that God has given to you is yours to treasure, and you have a responsibility to lavish upon her greater love than she would receive from her own mother or father. The bar is set high, especially if she is a child of God, because God deeply values and loves your wife.

The second marriage application takes us back to the idea of banners. Earlier in poem 7, we discovered that his banner over her was love; now in this poem, she is described as someone who is as awesome as an army with a banner. A banner represents who we are, and our banner should also be our pride and glory. In 1 Corinthians 11:7, Paul tells us that men are the glory of God, and that women are the glory of men. This means that, as men, our actions can either honor or tarnish the name of God. In Paul's culture, the action of a wife could equally either tarnish or honor the name of her husband. In the context of our present culture, everyone has a responsibility to bring honor or glory, and not shame, upon each other and God.

I've discussed this before, but it is important to entertain the question once again. We need to constantly ask and evaluate what the banner is that flies over our relationship and characterizes it from the rest. We are fortunate that in our culture, we no longer live in the age when life was all about pretense, status and protecting the family's name. However, it is important for us to realize that how we conduct ourselves in public does reflect upon our marriage partner and our children. Whether we like it or not, we have a reputation and/or a title, which is the banner that identifies us. It is important, for the sake of our families, that our banner brings honor to both God and our family.

**Exercise:** Ask your spouse to write out a word or phrase that best describes your most predominant character trait. Do the same for your spouse. Try to guess the word or phrase your spouse has written for you. Is it the name that you would want to be written on your banner? If not, what would you like your banner to say about you?

Begin this discussion with a time of prayer together where you praise God for each other. It is important for you to be aware before entering into this exercise that what your partner has to share may be difficult for you to accept. Therefore, make sure that you enter this discussion fully prepared, through prayer, to accept with grace the perception of your spouse and others. At the end of your conversation, create a banner that represents what you both want to be a description of the relationship of your marriage. After you have created the banner, try to make some plans to help you both grow in the area that you believe God wants you to grow in, so that you come closer to the ideal of your new banner. Keep your banner hanging somewhere as a reminder of who you want to be and your goals for achieving what you want to be.

**Allegorical thought:**

Begin by reading Revelation 21:1-2, 9-11, 22-27. In the above poem, the woman is described as being as beautiful as two cities. Likewise, in Revelation, the bride of Christ is referred to as the new city of Jerusalem. As the armies protect the city and fly a banner over it, so does God protect his bride, the church. In Revelation, the bride is described as the most beautiful. As the new heaven and the new earth, she is the culmination of all of God's creation. There is none other that rise above her.

As we look deeper into the new heaven and earth, we discover that there is both physical beauty and spiritual glory. For instance, no one who is impure can enter the city, because impurities are not allowed. It is interesting that in Ephesians 5:27, Paul talks about the bride (the church) as someone who is to be presented before God without spot or blemish so that she can be identified as one who is holy. Often, when we think about holiness, we assume that it is beyond our reach because holiness describes the character of God. However, God tells us to be holy in the same way that He is holy (1 Peter 1:16). It would be out of the character of God to ask us to accomplish something that is not within His ability to enable us to do.

**Exercise:** How is your holiness rating? Confession is good for the soul, but confession is also required for purification. Take some quiet time to come before God and, as the Psalmist requests of God, ask Him to search you and show you if there is anything that needs to be purified in your life. Since you are not perfect, expect God to reveal something that you need to address. Thank Him for what He has revealed to you, and then make plans to move forward with cleansing and with obedience in whatever way God asks you to respond.

# Poem 14
## Swept Away
## 6:11-12

> I went down to the nut orchard
> to look at the blossoms of the valley,
> to see whether the vines had budded,
> whether the pomegranates were in bloom.
> ¹² Before I was aware, my desire set me
> among the chariots of my kinsman, a prince.

When you read this poem in our English translations, it can be very confusing. Part of the challenge is that there is a disagreement as to whether it is the woman or the man who is talking. The NIV attributes this verse to the man, whereas the ESV, NLT and most other translations have the woman speaking. The most direct translation from the Hebrew interlinear Bible reads like this:

> *"I went down to the garden of nut-trees, to see the fruits of the ravine, to see whether the vine flowered and the pomegranates budded. I did not know, but my soul set me on the chariots of my princely people."*

If we read this poem in the figurative way, with the assumption that the woman is speaking, then the interpretation that some suggest may make some of you blush. They describe this poem as a very sexual vignette, where the woman is exploring the male genitalia of her husband and, as would be expected of any healthy man, her exploration quickly turns into a sexually physical and passionate experience, which she likens to a chariot ride.

It is interesting that the exact phrase; "see whether the vines have budded, whether the grape's blossoms have opened and pomegranates are in bloom" is also used in chapter 7:12. Pomegranates were considered a fertility fruit that were a natural aphrodisiac as well as a symbol of fertile soil. In the context of chapter 7, the phrase is used to describe the place and time where she will offer her sexual love to her beloved. This lends support to the above interpretation, especially if you happen to look at pictures of grape clusters, which, when hanging on the vine, appear to be very representative of male genitals. Grape clusters are often hidden behind a leaf, which can easily remind us of the couple in the garden or of many of the marble statues of nudes in Italy.

However, there is also the possibility of a deeper level of understanding here, which borders on an allegorical interpretation. It is interesting to note that in Numbers 13:23, both grapes and pomegranates were brought back by the spies for the purpose of showing the people the richness of the Promised Land. It would therefore be quite appropriate that these symbols be used in the metaphor of this poem to also represent promise, hope, wealth, fertility, and blessings, which are all from God's hand. Remember that the Promise Land was to be a foreshadowing of heaven. It was the restored place where God was to rule as king and provide his blessings to His people. It was also representative of Eden restored.

Before the Israelites entered into the Promised Land, Scripture tells us that the land, known as the land of Canaan, was defiled. Leviticus 18 describes a list of sexual sins, followed by comments in verses 24 & 25, which describe the Promised Land as a land defiled by the sexual sins of the people who lived there. Defilement means that the land is no longer pure, and because of this, it can no longer be used for sacred purposes. Therefore, it is important in the redemption story throughout Scripture to restore sexual purity to the land of promise. Verses like Deuteronomy 24:4 describe a divorce and marriage situation which is "detestable in the eyes of the Lord," followed by the admonishment that the people should not bring sin upon the land. Also Jeremiah 3:1&2, describes Israel as a prostitute and laments that her actions have defiled the land. As a result of the people being impure, they were eventually exiled from the land of promise.

Now in the Song of Songs, we have this contrast to the story of the defiled Promised Land. Love Redeemed allows the woman of this poem to enjoy the love of her husband, within the boundaries of sexual purity. Sexual love is restored, and all is as it was meant to be. The land has once again been purified.

**Marriage Application:**

There are several applications that can be made, depending on the translation you use and how you want to interpret the passage. The first application could be that Love Redeemed allows married couples to enjoy wild, passionate sex. For those of you who accept this application, I will let you have fun coming up with your own practical exercises to reinforce this application. Enjoy!

The second application may be that passionate feelings of the heart are difficult to control and may therefore, catch us by surprise. For your sake, I hope you do have some great moments and memories of spontaneity. Whether your relationship can be described as a casual stroll in the park or as a fast chariot ride may depend on your mood of the day. The important thing to remember is that God allows a lot of liberties in the marriage bed. There are actually very few 'don'ts'. The one 'do not' that is always expressed is, 'do not invite a third party'. I believe that this includes pornographic videos. The marriage bed is exclusive to one man and one woman enjoying great freedoms together as a married couple. When a couple remains within God's guidelines, they are free to pursue creative and passionate sexual intimacy without defiling the Promised Land, which Love Redeemed has sanctified.

**Exercise:** Spend some time talking to your partner about the sexual liberties you are comfortable with, and those that you are not comfortable with. Ask yourself, "Is my discomfort based upon valid reasons such as health concerns and physical pain? or, have I created boundaries that, like the Pharisees' rules for the Sabbath, go beyond God's intended freedom for sexual intimacy between married couples?" If there are areas that you are questioning, then do some research together. There are some really good Christian websites, blogs and books that offer clear sexual advice. As a general rule, if God doesn't specifically say, "Don't," then feel free to do, while remaining respectful of each other. Remember that sexual intimacy, even during the fun times, is meant to be an expression of gratitude and love to the other partner.

As I am writing this, a new movie has been introduced to the theatre that encourages couples to experiment with sadism and masochism (S&M). It may be just the hype of the movie, but I have been sensing that it is becoming more popular for couples to introduce practices of S&M into their sex life. In light of the comments that I have made earlier about sexual freedoms in a marriage, I would like to suggest extreme caution before venturing into S&M practices as this particular area of sexual interest emphasizes domination, pain and aggression, where pure sexual intimacy should be emphasizing the opposite message. I understand wanting to experiment with exercises such as wearing blindfolds to heighten the awareness of the other senses, but a line can easily be crossed which leads into activities that are dishonorable, disrespectful and harmful. Make sure that both of you agree on healthy, God honoring boundaries before venturing into experimenting with S&M.

**Allegorical Thought:**

Just like spontaneous, passionate sex, God should be expected to do the unexpected in an overpowering way. (Some of you may have trouble getting your head around that particular metaphor.) We cannot put God in a box, especially when it comes to the moving of the Spirit. Like the return of Christ, which Scripture clearly teaches will come unexpectedly "like a thief in the night", so other spiritual events can also happen quickly, and without warning. In Acts 2:1-4, Luke describes the followers of Jesus as casually gathering together in anticipation of the Holy Spirit when "'suddenly' there came from heaven a sound like a mighty rushing wind, and it filled the entire house where they were sitting. And divided tongues as of fire appeared to them and rested on each one of them." Even though Jesus told them to wait for the Spirit to come upon them, it seems that when it happened they were all taken by surprise. When God shows up in these unexpected ways, it is always spectacular.

We cannot plan our closest and most passionate moments with God. These moments will happen when we least expect them. However, if we desire times of strong spiritual connection with God, then we need to make sure that we are spending time in his presence. We also need to anticipate that there will be times when, like a chariot swooping in out of nowhere, (remember Elijah's experience) we are caught up in an amazing filling of the Spirit of God. Enjoy the moment!

**Exercise:** What would a powerful connection with the Spirit of God look like for you? Spend some time in quiet expectation, waiting for the Spirit of God to empower you. Since we cannot dictate our wishes upon God it may not happen as we request, but allowing yourself to fantasize about God filling your life with Himself is still a worthy exercise. Are you aware of any impurities that would keep this from happening? If so, confess them and cleanse the temple of God (1 Corinthians 6:12-20). Remember, the temple needs to be purified before God will fill it with His presence.

# Poem 15
## Part A– The dancer
## 6:13-7:5

Return, return, O Shulammite,
return, return, that we may look upon you.
Why should you look upon the Shulammite,
as upon a dance before two armies?
⁷ How beautiful are your feet in sandals,
O noble daughter!
Your rounded thighs are like jewels,
the work of a master hand.
² Your navel is a rounded bowl
that never lacks mixed wine.
Your belly is a heap of wheat,
encircled with lilies.
³ Your two breasts are like two fawns,
twins of a gazelle.
⁴ Your neck is like an ivory tower.
Your eyes are pools in Heshbon,
by the gate of Bath-rabbim.
Your nose is like a tower of Lebanon,
which looks toward Damascus.
⁵ Your head crowns you like Carmel,
and your flowing locks are like purple;
a king is held captive in the tresses.

This is another long song that could easily be broken down into 3 parts. I have chosen to divide it into 2 parts. The first part describes the dancer, and the second part, which I have called the dance, portrays how he desires to make love to the dancer. If I were to divide this into three parts, then the third part would be her invitation for him to enjoy her sexually and to enter into the dance as her partner. This is a very visual song, which uses a large variety of visual metaphors to describe her body, his sexual desire for her and their sexual intimacy together.

This song or poem is describing what the Greeks called "Eros" love, which some people may see as too shallow, lustful and surface-like in a proper relationship. However, it seems that God has designed our sexual nature to be triggered by all of our senses in a very erotic and pleasurable way. Therefore, we must not think of "Eros love" as too shallow or wrong. Instead, "Eros" must be balanced with "Agape" love, which is the deeper committed love that allows relationships to survive when "Eros" love wanes. In the Song of Songs, we are reminded in several poems that "Eros" love is emotionally powerful and therefore, must be kept in check. It should not be awakened until the couple is prepared for "Agape" love to be the binding commitment of the relationship. Song of Songs makes us aware that "Eros" love is a gift of God, which is also needed in a healthy marriage. It is important for married couples to acknowledge that passionate sex is part of the experiential joy that God wants them to experience as one of His blessings in their marriage.

The song starts off by describing a woman who has just danced for her lover. The way in which he describes her suggests that in all probability she would have just finished a belly dance, a common dance in the Middle East. This poem presents for the third time a description of the woman, but it is significant to note that this time, his description of her goes from her feet up to her head rather than from her head to her feet. In doing this, the poem once again tends to be counter-cultural since, as I have mentioned before, drawing attention to the feet in the Middle East is considered to be culturally shameful. Yet he begins his description of her by describing her feet as beautiful. This should remind us that "Naked and Unashamed" includes all body parts. Love Redeemed does not accept any cultural perceptions that certain body parts are to be shameful between a husband and wife. A dance typically involves the movement of feet, which is another reason that his attention is drawn to her feet.

The opening line of the poem is calling her back; likely she is being called back to center stage for applause or comments of gratitude and praise after the dance has been completed. The song gives you the impression that others have been watching the dance along with her husband. Since this is a song and not a description of an historical event, the writer has the poetic license to change the scenario from public to private without notice, which he seems to do later on in the poem.

The phrase translated "dance before two armies" is the Hebrew word "machaneh" which is literally used to describe an army camp, but can also be used figuratively to describe a group of dancers, or a group of angels or any group of people or animals. It is the same way that we use the word "troop" to describe a group of actors or a band or a group of soldiers. The ESV asks the question, "Why should you look", but the NLT has probably the best translation of this verse; "Why do you stare at this young Shulam, as she moves so gracefully between two lines of dancers?" This gives us the sense that there is a group of dancers, but that she is the lead dancer who is drawing the crowd's attention.

The word "Shulamite" is from the feminine form of Solomon. The word means "perfect one" or "woman of peace". If the word is being used figuratively, it does not require her to be from a particular village, but may simply suggest that she is his "perfect one". In my research, I could not find any group of people who were known as the Shulamites, nor was there a city or region known as Shulam. Therefore, it is very likely that this person is fictitious. The meaning of her name is more significant than ascribing her to a place. The fact that Shulamite is from the feminine form of Solomon may also raise the question of whether the use of the name Solomon is also more about the meaning of the name than about the king we associate with the name. We must also remember that Solomon was likely a common name and therefore, King Solomon was not the only person who had that name. With this being the case, it may be a wrong assumption that the first verse of the book is talking about King Solomon.

If the use of these names in the Song of Songs is more about the significance of the meaning of the name rather than about the connection to a particular person, then it would mean that our two characters are "man of peace" or a perfect man and "woman of peace" or a perfect woman. This meaning could easily draw us back to the pre-fallen condition of Adam and Eve or be representative of all couples that have experienced forgiveness through the redemption of Christ and are living as new creations in Christ. Love Redeemed has the ability to create relationships where the man and woman are the perfect couple, and the relationship is marked by peace and the blessings of God.

Verse 1 of chapter 7 begins a description of the dancer. As already mentioned, the description of the woman goes from her feet up to her head, which is really unusual, since bringing attention to the feet in the Middle East is socially improper. However, Love Redeemed, in seeking to bring us back to the state of "naked and unashamed" does not allow for any undesirable or shameful parts. Therefore, her feet are noble and beautiful, especially in sandals. From her feet, we move to a description of her thighs or hips, which is another part of her body that has not been previously described in the Song of Songs.

The depiction of her navel and belly has a feast theme, with wine and bread tastefully garnished with flowers, all of which are, within this culture, associated with fertility and eroticism. The Hebrew words translated as 'navel' and 'belly' are also used in other poetry of the same era as euphemisms for the female genitals, in the same way that my wife used the word 'bottom' when talking to our young daughters. (In those days, anything below the belly button that needed to be wiped was described as the bottom.) The idea that is being portrayed in the poem is that the woman's body provides a banquet for him of everything that is needed to fulfill his hunger and thirst (sexually). This banquet also includes the ambiance of beautifully displayed lilies. It is significant to note that she not only provides for his needs in regards to his sexual appetite, but that she also does it with attention to presentation. We are not talking about a snack in front of the TV. This is a full banquet that has been carefully laid out with full attention to every detail. (See marriage application discussion related to poem 7)

The description of the rest of her body is very similar to previous descriptions. There is a slight variation in how he portrays her neck from 4:4, but it is the same sentiment. The illustration of her eyes has changed from the dove metaphor to the pools of Heshbon. It is possible that Heshbon is the city mentioned in Numbers 21, which was captured by Israel when the Amorites refused to give them passage through their land and instead attacked the nation. However, the meaning of the word is "power of reason" or "purposeful thinking", so it is possible, like her name, that the description of her eyes speaks of her character more than their appearance. With regard to the pools of Hesbon, not much is known today of the pools. They were probably used for bathing and, because of their location by the gate, they would be a welcome invitation for travelers entering the city. This could easily suggest that her eyes were very attractive and welcoming maybe even alluring.

In reference to her nose, it is clear that prominent noses were looked upon as beautiful, which goes to show how much our culture has to say about what we perceive as beautiful. The tower of Lebanon was a watch tower with the purpose of watching for enemy activity that might come from Damascus. Therefore, once again, the discussion of her nose being like a watchtower could have more to say about her alertness and her sense of purpose (no pun intended) then it does about her appearance.

Verse 5 begins the description of her head, which, in the Middle East, is a person's crowning glory. He compares her head to Mount Carmel, which was a well known mountain that had a very beautiful forest with rich vegetation. In a culture that is highly dependent upon agriculture, any land that is extremely fertile is seen as a land that has God's blessing. As a result, the fertile mountain of Carmel also hosted an altar, which made it both beautiful and sacred. It is also interesting to discover that the Hebrew spelling for "Karmel" is only one letter different from the spelling of the word purple, which is "Karmil". The color purple was always associated with royalty, and Mount Carmel was surrounded by the cities that were involved in the purple dye industry. So, with both "Karmel" and "Karmil" reflecting a sense of sacredness and royalty, the poet is given an opportunity to use a beautiful play on words in describing the glory, royalty and sacredness of her head.

Speaking of play on words, in the English translation there also appears to be a play on words between "locks of hair" and "locks that hold someone captive". Her locks of hair have captivated the king. Hair was considered to be a very seductive part of the female anatomy, which is why in later years a woman is required to keep her hair covered except in the presence of her husband. The seductiveness of a woman's hair is part of Paul's concern in 1 Corinthians 11:6-7.

As with most of the Song of Songs, it is clear that the lover who is describing his beloved woman sees her as being very attractive in a majestic way. In this case, she is so beautiful and majestic that she is able to captivate the king's attention. Once again, this does not necessarily refer to King Solomon. As we have seen throughout the Song of Songs, her beloved is a king to her and she is queen to him. Using the imagery of king and queen is a way of symbolizing respect and admiration, beauty, power, glory and even chivalry.

**Marriage Application:**

Since this is our third description of the woman, we have already talked a lot about physical beauty and the need to share with our wives our appreciation for their body and character beauty. In this poem, we are reminded once again that in a healthy, intimate marriage, we should be free to be naked and unashamed. It is important that we see and experience our partner's body as a gift from God that appeals to all of our five senses. In a marriage, there should not be any part of the body, which is hidden from the other due to shame or embarrassment.

**Exercise:** As you are lying naked beside each other, share with your partner how their body delights all of your senses. Talk about the parts of their body that you love to touch, and describe the sensation. What are the touch sensations that your partner enjoys? Light touch, firm touch, caress, blowing your warm breath on them or using a feather? Enjoy experimenting with touch: feel free to get creative. Do the same for your other senses: talk about how their body appeals to your senses of taste, sight, smell and even sound.

**Allegorical Thought:**

God invites us into His presence, and He desires us to be aware of Him at all times. In school, the teacher may have told you to pay attention before he/she was about to teach you something important. This required you to stop all other thoughts and focus on what the teacher wanted to say. Paying attention to God is slightly different. God allows you to let your focus go wherever it might want to go, but requires you to ask the Spirit of God to show you God's presence in every thought or experience. In this way, you can learn to enjoy the presence of God in the simple things of life. He will begin to reveal Himself in unique ways as you discover the world through all of your senses. The eye will see God as creator in all of your surroundings. The ear will appreciate the sound of nature, music, laughter, and even silence as the voice of God. Smells will also help you to reflect on the One who created beautiful aromas for the good things He wants to draw you closer to and repugnant smells for things that we would be better to stay clear of. The taste of food and fine wine will draw us into an appreciation for His gift that allows eating to be such a delight. And finally, touch, warmth in the winter and coolness in the summer, a hug from a mother and a kiss from a lover-all of these touch sensations are equally gifts from the Creator, and represent His power, wisdom, care and commitment.

**Exercise:** If you are married, take the exercise from the marriage application to another level and use it as a worship experience to thank God for allowing you to enjoy your partner's body through all of your senses. While doing this, give praise to God for His creation.

If you are single, go for a walk with God and seek to awaken your senses. Pack some natural snacks-fruit, nuts or veggies that you enjoy. As you walk, allow yourself to be awakened to the experience of the senses. Praise God for what you are able to see, hear, touch, smell and taste. Allow the Spirit of God to speak to your emotions through these discoveries. Some things that you see may draw you into intercessory prayer, other things may encourage you to sing or to respond in different expressions of gratitude and pleasure. Enjoy this walk as a time of feeling the beauty and closeness of God's presence. (The appendix provides a plan for a prayer retreat that awakens all of your senses to God's presence. I would encourage you to try some of those ideas in this exercise.)

# Poem 15
## Part B – The Dance
## 7:6-13

⁶ How beautiful and pleasant you are,
O loved one, with all your delights!
⁷ Your stature is like a palm tree,
and your breasts are like its clusters.
⁸ I say I will climb the palm tree
and lay hold of its fruit.
Oh may your breasts be like clusters of the vine,
and the scent of your breath like apples,
⁹ and your mouth like the best wine.
It goes down smoothly for my beloved,
gliding over lips and teeth.
¹⁰ I am my beloved's,
and his desire is for me.
¹¹ Come, my beloved,
let us go out into the fields
and lodge in the villages;
¹² let us go out early to the vineyards
and see whether the vines have budded,
whether the grape blossoms have opened
and the pomegranates are in bloom.
There I will give you my love.
¹³ The mandrakes give forth fragrance,
and beside our doors are all choice fruits,
new as well as old,
which I have laid up for you, O my beloved.

Part 2 of poem 15, begins with a summary of the previous verses and provides an introduction to the verses that follow, so verses 6 to 9 become what is known as a bridge. This is why some commentators would see verses 6 to 9 as a separate poem. The poet begins poem 15 by describing the woman's beauty, but in part 2 he takes his description a step further by sharing how her beauty arouses her husband's desire for sexual intimacy. She is like a magnet to him: he sees her and he is drawn to her. In a powerfully poetical way, we have the progression of foreplay being acted out in verses 6 to 9.

The Hebrew word for palm tree is the word 'Tamar', which interestingly enough is associated with beautiful women in the Old Testament. In Genesis 38, Tamar is the woman who seduces Judah, her father-in-law, into lying with her and making her pregnant. In 2 Samuel 13, Tamar is David's daughter with whom, her brother Amnon wants to enjoy sexual intimacy because he is so obsessed with her beauty. He is so lustfully taken with her that he develops a plan that forces her into sexual submission. Also, in 2 Samuel 14:27, Absalom had a beautiful daughter who was named Tamar. So the *double entendre* here suggests that she is a beautiful woman, like a palm tree?

Originally, I thought that the poet was talking about a coconut palm tree, but coconuts don't grow in clusters. Then, through Google Images, I discovered date palm trees, which grow large clusters of dates that do somewhat resemble a woman's breast. So, if you look up a picture of date clusters, you will have a clearer understanding of the metaphor that is being described in this poem. The husband's intention is to not just admire the fruit of his palm tree, but to climb the tree and take hold of its fruit (invoking the sense of touch). Then he imagines that his clusters of dates are grapes instead of dates. Now his sense of taste is also very much engaged in this adventure. Finally, his sense of smell becomes part of the experience as the scent of her breath reminds him of apples and the best of wine. Note how this poem continues the banquet metaphor that is begun when he describes her belly and navel.

It is easy to conclude that his desire, or better said, hunger, for her is strong, and as we will soon see, her invitation to him is equally inviting and welcoming. In the next verse, the feast is fully prepared and so she gives herself completely over to his ravishing appetite for his sexual delights. In the remaining verses of this love song, we have her invitation for him to enter into her garden of love and to enjoy the Eden of delights that she has prepared for him.

It is interesting that the word translated as 'desire' within this poem is only used 3 times within Scripture. One of those times is in Genesis 3:16 where part of the curse is for a woman's 'desire' to be for her husband. In this verse, however, the word 'desire' is used in a positive sense, where "his 'desire' is for her" (as it should be). In the Song of Songs, Love Redeemed reverses the curse of Genesis 3, if only for a short period of time, during moments of sexual intimacy: 'desire' is no longer a curse but a beautiful longing that is fulfilled.

In the poetic nature of the Song of Songs, the countryside and garden setting are always connected with joyful togetherness as a couple. The countryside represents the return back to the place of Eden that was perfectly experienced by man and woman before the Fall. The city, on the other hand, is depicted as a place of alienation, which is lacking the close intimacy that the couple desires. In the city scenes, there is always a desperate search for the lost lover or a call from one lover to the next to be reunited. For this reason, there is some confusion as to why the English translations translate the Hebrew word in verse 11 as "villages". This word, I discovered, could just as easily be translated as "henna bush", which seems to me to be a better fit.[12]

The henna plant provides an ink that was traditionally used to add artistic designs to the body, especially surrounding weddings in the Middle East. Just before the wedding day, there is something known as a henna party, to which only family members and close friends are invited. During this party, which includes much dancing and music, the grandmother brings out a dish with henna ink in it, as well as lit candles. The henna ink is used by the grandmother to stain the palms of the bride and groom as she blesses them. With this event in mind, and considering the context of this poem, I would suggest that henna fields, which are representative of marriage blessings, would be a more accurate translation than the word 'villages'.

Verse 12 repeats the wording of 6:11 (poem 14), where we have a clear word picture being used to describe the place and/or time for sexual intimacy. I have provided a full description in my discussion of poem 14 of the significance of this metaphor. In summary, I believe that the wording represents the fertile blessings that God gives to the married couple, which allows them to enjoy the pleasures of sexual intimacy and the resulting gift of

---

[12] Tremper Longman III, *The New International Commentary on the Old Testament – Song of Songs* (Grand Rapids: Eerdmans, 2001) p.200.

children. In reference to the Promised Land, which I talk about in poem 14, the wording also refers to sexual purity along with sexual liberty and enjoyment in marriage.

The mandrake root, which we see mentioned in verse 13, is often shaped like a human body and in Genesis 30:14-16, it was used as a natural fertility plant that Rachel took in order to conceive. In the Middle East, the ability to conceive and have children is recognized as a special blessing from God. A barren woman is seen as someone whom God has cursed and, therefore, it would not be uncommon for her to be shunned by the members of her community.

'Door' is a word to describe portal or entrance way. It is often understood as the entrance to a place or situation of opportunity as in our use of the phrase "doorway to opportunity". In this case, it may also be describing the various portals of the body, which are actively engaged during lovemaking. Whatever the situation may be, the concept is that there are great blessings that lie waiting at the entrance. Some of these blessings will be new experiences, and some will be old and traditionally familiar in a comforting and welcoming way.

**Marriage Application:**

The sexual experience is meant to draw upon all of our senses in a very positive manner. Positive enjoyment of the senses feeds positive emotional experiences. In the beginning, before the Fall, God created a Garden of Eden that was completely pleasurable to all of the senses of man. As a result, the emotional experiences of man were also pleasurable. Adam and Eve enjoyed life in every way imaginable through their five senses and through the resulting positive emotions. After the Fall, however, their senses began to experience ugliness in addition to beauty. Their emotions, in turn, began to experience negative thoughts; fears, anger and so on, whereas they had only previously known pleasure.

Love Redeemed restores the beauty; it helps us to focus our senses and our emotions on that which is pleasurable. The Fruit of the Spirit, as described in Galatians 5:22-23, reflects only positive emotions and attitudes. When you are making love together in your marriage relationship, the experience should give you a foreshadowing of the experience of heaven, where all negative emotional and sensory experiences will be removed, and you will experience only the joy and pleasure of your senses.

Love making within the marriage should provide a Garden of Eden experience within your world of chaos. In a way, it should be a retreat from the ugliness of life's situations that you face daily. It should be a gift that you give to yourself and to your marriage partner that helps you both to escape any troubling circumstances that you are facing in life. It is, therefore, important for couples to getaway from time to time for a Promised Land or Eden experience. When you do this, it helps to keep the marriage alive, and it also provides an escape where, for a moment in time, all can be emotionally pleasurable as a reminder of what God has in store for us in eternity.

**Exercise:** In poem 8, I encouraged couples to get away and enjoy time together. Once again, I would encourage you to get away as a couple for the purpose of enjoying the gift of sexual intimacy. This time, when you go, pack items that will help you to appeal to all of your senses. You can use your imagination here, but to help you out, I would suggest items such as massage oil for touch, music, maybe a scented candle or incense, and don't forget to plan for taste. Plan this together; use your imagination, give yourselves lots of sense-awakening liberties, and enjoy your time together, stimulating the senses. Consider this time together as a love banquet or feast. Indulge to the fullest.

**Allegorical Thought:**

This section of the poem is all about a lover enjoying the sensual pleasures of his wife's body. We have already explored how God wants us to experience Him through our senses by focusing on His creation. However, God also wants us to experience a Spirit-filled life that allows us to see opportunity and potential, understanding and compassion even in the things that are ugly to our senses - those things that often trigger negative emotions. I know that this poem does not address negative feelings, but I thought that it would be interesting to explore this area of life as well.

In the book, <u>Sensible Shoes</u> by Sharon Garlough Brown, professor Allen makes the following comment to one of his students, "Remember, Charissa – the things that annoy, irritate, and disappoint us have just as much power to reveal the truth about ourselves as anything else. Learn to linger with what provokes you. You may just find the Spirit of God moving there."[13] Sometimes the way that we react to the things that provoke us keeps us from experiencing the pleasures of life. When we focus on the root of the negative feelings and emotions within us, we will often discover a judgmental attitude, fear or unforgiveness, summarized as 'pride'. When we learn to

---

[13]  Sharon Garlough Brown, *Sensible Shoes* (Downers Grove: Intervarsity Press, 2013) p.80.

deal with the pride that allows our negative emotions to rule our hearts and minds, we will free ourselves to enjoy more of the pleasures in life; then we will truly be free to dance and to love and to be the lover that is fully naked and unashamed.

**Exercise:** Take the time to consider a behavior that your partner or a friend does that provokes you. This time, however, don't let your thought life conjure up emotions that produce anger, frustration or other negative feelings. Instead, allow the Spirit of God to take you into a deeper consideration of what is at the root of your provocation. Are you embarrassed, or afraid of being embarrassed? Are you seeing yourself as a better person? What is the belief that justifies your right to be provoked? Does this belief come from a pure source or is it a false belief? How does pride relate to your feelings? Is God trying to make you aware of an idol in your life?

After the Spirit of God reveals what is in your heart that allows you to have these negative thoughts and feelings, deal with the heart issue in whatever way the Spirit guides you. Maybe you will need to ask your partner for forgiveness, or maybe you will need to practice the art of grace, mercy and forgiveness.

# Concluding Poems

In chapter 8, the Song of Songs ends with a series of 4 poems that speak to the fact that we do not live in a perfect world and therefore, there are cultural challenges that Love Redeemed needs to overcome. In poem 16, the cultural situation of our imperfect world requires us to live within the boundaries that are placed upon relationship intimacy. Although the true redemption of love would set us free from these restrictions if we were living in the Garden of Eden where all was right and pure, the fact is that we do not live in a perfect environment, and so, the freedoms of love need to be restrained for our protection, by the rules of our society.

In Poem 17 we have a discussion of covenant commitment, which is required in order for a couple to conquer the challenges that they will face within a marriage. 'Eros' or sexual love, which is the love so often described in Song of Songs, takes second place in this poem to 'Agape' love, which is described as the power over all other forces. Love Redeemed looks to the redemption of Christ to provide a solid commitment for the challenges that marriages will face.

In Poem 18, the subject of keeping chaste before marriage is addressed. At the time when this poem was written, it was of high value for a woman to enter her first marriage as a virgin. However, in much of our present world today, this value has actually been reversed so that youth are now seen to be socially immature and backward if they maintain their virginity until marriage. In this poem, Love Redeemed asks us to act in a matter that is contrary to the present norms of our society in order to maintain what God values for marriage and sexual intimacy.

Finally, in Poem 19, the subject of polygamy is raised. This was a real problem during the time of King Solomon, and especially for King Solomon himself. The poem speaks to the value of the woman and to the fact that she should not be treated as property or as a pawn to be used for political gain. Love Redeemed reminds us that in a marriage relationship the feelings and wishes of the woman are of equal value to those of the man. We are also reminded that marriage is to be a commitment with pure motives that align with God's family values.

# Poem 16
## Wishful Thinking
## 8:1-4

> Oh that you were like a brother to me
> who nursed at my mother's breasts!
> If I found you outside, I would kiss you,
> and none would despise me.
> ²I would lead you and bring you
> into the house of my mother—
> she who used to teach me.
> I would give you spiced wine to drink,
> the juice of my pomegranate.
> ³His left hand is under my head,
> and his right hand embraces me!
> ⁴I adjure you, O daughters of Jerusalem,
> that you not stir up or awaken love
> until it pleases.

This poem starts out as a dream or wishful imagining of the woman. It speaks about what she would like, but not about what she receives. To understand her desire, it is necessary to understand the Middle Eastern cultural restraints regarding couples in public. In that culture, there was more public liberty allowed for a sister towards her brother than for a wife towards her husband. For instance, it was acceptable for a woman to kiss her brother in public, but not her husband. Likewise, it was acceptable for a sister to hold her brother's hand in public, but not for a wife to hold her husband's hand. Among some Islamic groups today, it is not even acceptable for a wife to look at her husband in a public place, let alone speak to him when others are present. We know from 1 Corinthians 14:33-35 that a similar cultural restraint was happening in the first century church.

In the Garden of Eden, there were no cultural restraints against women or against public displays of affection, but unfortunately we do not live in the Garden of Eden. Instead, we live in the reality of our world where we all have cultural guidelines and, since we do not live in a perfect world where all people act in a righteous way towards each other, these restraints are actually good things. They protect us from those who would abuse the privilege of freedom. In the same way, Adam and Eve were removed from the garden for their own protection, so that they could not eat from the tree of life and thereby live forever in their state of sinfulness. If we lived in a world where life was pure and undefiled, public displays of affection would not be a problem, but in our world it is a problem, so our society provides us with rules.

When the woman uses the phrase "I would...", she is not thinking in terms of how she would treat a brother, but in terms of wishing she had the cultural freedom to publicly express her love to the person she loves. In the Hebrew, there is also a play on words in this poem as the phrase "I would give you to drink" sounds very close to the phrase "I would kiss you". Clearly, the kiss that she would offer to her husband is significantly different from the one she would give to her brother. The suggestion of offering spiced wine and pomegranate juice in the context of the Song of Songs is likely related to sexual intimacy. However, we can only guess at the exact meaning of this sentence.

In verse 4, we have a phrase that we have read several times before. This time, it is missing the line "I charge you by the gazelles and by the does of the field". However, the same sentiment is presented: do not awaken love until it so desires to be awakened. There is a time for everything, including a time for awakening sexual love. Sexual love, as many of us have discovered, is a very powerful emotion that should be liberally experienced (within its proper context), but it must also be controlled during those times and in those places where it is inappropriate to display this kind of affection. The warning is that the power of "Eros" love is difficult to keep in check. In fact, many lovers have not been able to control their physical passions towards each other. This poem, therefore, addresses the reality that our responsibility to society, God's guidelines and our family's values provides boundaries, which may be at odds with our sexual desires. It is not wrong to feel the tension between cultural boundaries and our sexual desires. However, it is always necessary to accept those boundaries and submit to them, especially outside of marriage and when we are not in a place where we can enjoy couple privacy. In other words, this song expresses the sentiment, "Get a room", as it speaks to this married couple that is overwhelmed by the power of "Eros" love.

**Marriage Application:**

It is important that couples do not flaunt their affection for each other in ways that are embarrassing to the public. Flirt with each other (Why not?), but do it in a way that respects the people around you. It is important for husbands and wives to publicly reflect their love and respect for each other, but only in appropriate ways that are not only accepted by society, but also admired. Couples also need to find adequate private time for each other. This may be difficult in certain circumstances, but where there is a will, I believe that they will always find a way.

**Exercise:** Consider how your public interaction with your partner speaks about your relationship. What appropriate gestures of affection (holding hands, one arm hugs, positive eye contact, kiss on the cheek and words of affirmation) are you using that show the world that you admire and respectfully love your mate? You may also ask if you are acting inappropriately in public. The flip side of the coin is to also take inventory of the body language and verbal dialogue that may suggest to your friends that your intimacy could use some enrichment.

**Allegorical Thought:**

Jesus taught that public worship also has boundaries. In Matthew 6:6, Jesus reminds us that we need to have times of private prayer. Intimate times with God should not necessarily be in view of the public eye. Yes, we need to worship God in a way that expresses to those around us that we have a love relationship with God, but when those around us are uncomfortable with our worship, then we need to check our motives. How do we justify allowing others to feel uncomfortable with our worship activities? The unity of worship requires a standard that everyone involved is comfortable with expressing. On another note, we need to ask ourselves if we are embarrassed about expressions of worship that are okay. Finding a balance point that gives you the freedom to worship fully but non-offensively may simply be a matter of watching how those around you worship. If there isn't at least a handful of people expressing worship in the manner you would like, then my suggestion is to show restraint when you are with that group.

**Exercise:** How do you express worship? Do you have personal boundaries in place that keep you from expressing certain forms of worship, which would cause those around you to feel uncomfortable? The apostle Paul addresses this concern in 1 Corinthians chapter 14. I would encourage you to read over this chapter and then consider if your worship aligns with all of Paul's guidelines. You may need to consider moving some of your public practices of worship to your own private prayer closet.

# Poem 17
## Redemption
## 8:5-7

Who is that coming up from the wilderness,
leaning on her beloved?
Under the apple tree I awakened you.
There your mother was in labor with you;
there she who bore you was in labor.
⁶Set me as a seal upon your heart,
as a seal upon your arm,
for love is strong as death,
jealousy is fierce as the grave.
Its flashes are flashes of fire,
the very flame of the Lord.
⁷Many waters cannot quench love,
neither can floods drown it.
If a man offered for love
all the wealth of his house,
he would be utterly despised.

The beauty of this poem is that it speaks very powerfully through its metaphors of Love's Redeeming qualities. For instance, it is significant that the couple is coming out of the desert or wilderness. A common metaphor in Scripture for redemption is that of a journey from the wilderness or desert into the Promised Land. The Israelites are an example of this, as they were required to go through a wilderness experience before arriving at the place of promise that God had chosen for them. We see in this verse that the couple is arm in arm; she is leaning upon him as they come out of the wilderness together, which speaks to the unity and intimacy of the couple. They symbolically represent a couple that is walking out of the wilderness, because their love for each other has been rescued and redeemed.

The second half of verse 5 describes a process related to giving birth. The word translated "awakened" or "roused" is actually the word that is used for arousal, which is the beginning of the birth process. Arousal is followed by conception, which eventually, over the course of time, is followed by the delivery of a child. The NLT adds the words "in great pain" which are not part of the text, but by adding these words the NLT provides us with a reminder of the Genesis 3 curse. In this Song, each of these events takes place under the apple tree. Clearly, the apple tree expresses a "Garden of Eden" experience, reflective of the blessings of God, as opposed to a wilderness experience.

In an ironic way, this poem may also remind us of the Sunday school pictures we were shown, as children, of Adam and Eve naked under an apple tree, about to eat of its fruit. The Latin word for "apple" and "evil" is the same, so the early Christian community traditionally associated the fruit that Eve gave Adam with the apple. If it is truly the case that the apple tree is representative of the tree of the knowledge of good and evil (which I highly doubt), then it is significant in this poem that it is under the apple tree where true love is once again awakened and a commitment between the couple is established. Although it was not likely on the mind of the poet, I thought that this was an interesting comparison. In this poem, it is under the apple tree that love is redeemed. Traditionally speaking, it was the apple, which introduced death to mankind. Significantly, in this poem, it is under the apple tree that new life has been given, which creates for us a beautiful picture of Love Redeemed.

Verse 5 also reminds me of Paul's summary in 1 Corinthians 11:12 "For as woman came from man, so also man is born of woman. But everything comes from God." The first half of Paul's statement tells us that the first woman came from man, but the second half makes it clear that every man from then on has come from a woman. Both men and women are required to produce new life. They are both equally a part of the new life experience, but God the Redeemer is the true Provider of life.

Another aspect of this verse is the fulfillment of God's command to be fruitful and multiply. It is only through the experience of sexual intimacy that this command is capable of being obeyed. The punishment for the original sin of Adam and Eve included both death and their relationship breakdown. However, the continuation of life is designed to be perpetuated through a deep, intimate relationship that is culminated in love expressed through the sexual intimacy between a husband and wife. Therefore, the redemption that allows for broken relationships to be restored also allows for new life to be conceived.

**Allegorical Thought and Marriage Application:**

In a mystical way God provides redemption for the world through Mary being conceived by the Holy Spirit of God, which allows her to give birth to a Savior who then brings total redemption to mankind. In a similar way, God allows believers today to experience a fullness of life in their spiritual person, through the filling of the Holy Spirit. Part of our redemption is a day-to-day experience whereby we are being filled with the Holy Spirit of God, which then allows us to produce the fruit of the Spirit.

In another metaphor describing redemption, Jesus likened Salvation to that of being born again. Therefore, the idea of conception and the filling of the Holy Spirit are related to new life and the conquest of death. The filling of the Spirit also releases us from the bondage of sin thus providing us with the freedom of Salvation (Galatians 5). Sexual intimacy in marriage can therefore be a reminder of the greater redemption story.

**Exercise:** In this exercise I would like to combine the exercise of allegorical thought with marriage application. Communion in church is an exercise that asks us to participate in the remembrance of what Christ did for us on the cross. With the same mind-set, the next time you and your spouse make love, take the time to remind each other of the way in which sexual intimacy is reflective of the redemption story. Your act of love towards one another is symbolic of breaking the curse of selfishness and hatred towards one another, and is also capable of producing new life through your unity.

**Back to Verse 6:**

The beginning of verse 6 calls for commitment. This is actually the first verse in the Song of Songs that speaks of love in the deeper context of commitment. A seal always represents the approval of a vow. It is the final act that says, "I agree to this decision." Today, it is like signing your name to a contract. There are two seals that are requested in this song: one on the heart and one on the arm. The heart represents our will and our emotions. The arm represents our actions, strength and ability. In this poem, the woman is calling for a strong commitment from her lover, which leads us to the question, why? The answer is that death is a strong opponent to love. Therefore, the power of love, represented by the seal on his arm, requires all of its strength to combat death. Love's jealousy (emotion) is also as unyielding as the grave; therefore, love that is represented by the seal of his heart is also required in order to battle the stronghold of the grave.

The structure of these lines is what is known as parallelism, where the second line is basically saying the same thing as the first line, but in a way that strengthens the concept being presented. In this case, love and jealousy are understood to be the same, just as death and the grave provide a similar meaning. Often, we think of the word "jealousy" in a negative way, but the Bible refers to God as a jealous God. When it comes to protecting a covenant relationship, jealousy is a positive emotion (guarding the seal of the heart), which leads to actions (defending by the seal of the arm) that seek to protect the relationship and the covenant. It is okay for God to be jealous whenever we turn away from him and go after other relationships.

We may discover that God's jealousy initially feels like punishment, but it was one of the motivators that gave God the desire to redeem man from his sin. For a deeper Scriptural reflection, you may consider the voice of God in Deuteronomy 32:21-22. "They have made me jealous with what is no god; they have provoked me to anger with their idols. So I will make them jealous with those who are no people; I will provoke them to anger with a foolish nation." God knows that if we are going to enjoy a fulfilling life, it can only happen by staying true to a relationship with him that is free from all other gods (idols). In the same way that God's jealousy seeks to protect and restore his covenantal relationship, it is okay for a husband to be jealous if someone is attempting to steal his wife. When an outsider or a spouse attempts to breakup a covenant relationship, jealousy is called upon as a powerful stimulus to protect the relationship from death.

## Marriage Application:

As already pointed out, love is a very powerful motivator and emotion, which should not be awakened too soon. The kind of love that is being described in the Song of Songs should also be controlled so that it is kept within the context of a marriage. This love is vulnerable because of our sin nature, and so it is important to jealously guard the seal of our commitment to one another. This means that the marriage partners always need to be alert and vigilant for whatever might want to interfere with the commitment and seek to attack or kill the relationship.

Relationship attacks may not always be as obvious as an outsider attempting to steal your spouse. For instance, any activity that tends to isolate or alienate a marriage partner so that he or she feels alone instead of in a partnership opens the door to strangers stepping in to fill the void. Examples of what I'm talking about include time commitments outside of the home such as jobs, volunteering, and other activities that don't include your spouse. Often these activities are both necessary and okay to do alone within normal daily activities, but if they go beyond what your spouse considers to be reasonable time allocations for these tasks, then as a couple you need to address the issue. Do not let quality couple time be robbed by good activities. It is also important for couples to consider the use of their time together at home. Are you reserving adequate time for your partner, or are the TV, jobs around the house, and the children robbing you and your mate of couple intimacy? Once, again reality requires that a balance be struck between household tasks and spending time with your partner.

A final way to steal from each other is the failure to reconcile when you hurt the bond of your partner relationship. Throughout the day, a couple has many relationship choices to make. Some of those choices will drive a wedge in the relationship and will emotionally separate you as a couple. Other choices will act as a bond. It is important to watch out for the times when you create a wedge, and to act to quickly remove it. Life is too short to live together in an attitude of resentment towards your spouse. Keep times of unreconciled relationship differences short so that you do not become vulnerable to the affections of a third party. Wedges cause a relationship to slowly die.

**Exercise:** Spend some time discussing the above with your spouse. Are there things you are doing that create too much 'alone' time for your partner? If there are, attempt to do some brainstorming that could lead to a solution. Be vigilant this week to notice the times when you create an emotional wedge within the relationship, and then quickly take action to remove this wedge so that healing can take place.

**Allegorical Thought:**

Love and Death are seen throughout the redemption story as powerful forces that are at war with each other. Jesus' death on the cross was an act of jealous love for His people. This expression of Jesus' love required the act of dying in order to conquer the curse of death and bring life. So in the crucifixion of Jesus, we see two very powerful forces: death working to defeat redemption, and love working to provide redemption.

**Exercise:** Read and meditate on John 14:12-13 and John 10:17-18. Consider the love that Jesus has shown to you by laying down His life. Praise Him for His love and redemption.

**Back to Verse 6b & 7:**

In the latter part of verse 6, we have another set of parallel forces being described. First, is the force of fire, which both destroys and purifies. Fire also describes both the passion of love as well as the rage of anger. These can be two very different but yet similarly powerful emotions. Along with fire is the power of water. In verse 7, 'waters' are parallel to 'floods' in the same way as 'quench' is to 'drown'. Love, however, is able to rise above the destruction of water since the power of love's flame cannot be quenched, nor can it be drowned. The flame of love, therefore, has the power to overcome the flood of waters.

It is significant to note that waters are often used in the Bible to symbolize chaos, disorder, evil forces and even death (Psalm 74:13, Isaiah 27:1).

- It was water that destroyed the world through the flood.
- It was water that destroyed Pharaoh and his army.
- It is out of the water that the beast of Revelation will appear.
- It was storms on the water that Jesus calmed.
- It was in water where Jonah, in his sin, was swallowed by a sea creature.
- It is into the depths of the sea that the sins of man will be cast (Micah 7:19).
- Out of water the world was formed (2 Peter 3:5). Compare with Genesis 1:2.

Up to this point in this poem, we have the requirement of commitment or the seal of the covenant of marriage providing love with the power to conquer both death and waters, which are both symbols of evil forces. However, there is more to consider than these two outside evil forces: there is also the selfish nature of man himself, and so, the poet ends the poem with the statement that love cannot be purchased. In Acts 8:18-19, Simon the sorcerer offered the apostles money in order to be able to give to people the power and gifts of the Holy Spirit, because he recognized the Spirit of God as a unique and desirable power. The apostles quickly recognized Simon's improper motives and rebuked him for wanting this gift. Wherever there is power, the selfishness of man will want to purchase it. Since this poem is about the power of a committed love that is capable of overcoming the forces of evil, it therefore seems prudent to the poet that he would also warn against the idea of trying to purchase such a power as love. Love that is a true relational commitment cannot be purchased, nor can it be owned.

**Marriage Application:**

Love Redeemed does not carry a monetary price tag. There are many applications that we can draw from this statement of truth. For instance, our motivation for marriage should have nothing to do with monetary gain. In our North American culture, this idea has pretty much ceased, but it is still alive and significant in many other cultures.

Secondly, sexual pleasure received through the offering of gifts does not come close to representing true love. In a healthy marriage relationship, sex should not have a price tag. A wife should not feel compelled to have sex with her husband, simply because he has spent money on her or because he is her financial provider. Likewise, a wife should not use sexual favors to bribe her husband into doing tasks. This misuse of sex tarnishes the purity of love in a covenant relationship. Sex that is purchased is not an expression of true love.

Thirdly, one of the top three reasons for struggles in marriages is financial problems. It is important to make sure that the glue that holds your marriage together is not related to how well your investments are doing or how well you are managing your budget. Be careful that money management issues are not allowed to drive a wedge into your relationship intimacy.

**Exercise:** Time to ask the question, "Is money destroying your intimacy?" If it is, then you may need to get some counseling on how to get your finances in order. Discuss with your spouse how to keep your relationship protected from money matters that tend to create a wedge in your marital intimacy. Value your love much higher than you do your wealth.

**Allegorical Thought:**

The New Testament Scriptures speak twice of fire being quenched. Ephesians 6:16 tells us that our faith is capable of acting as a shield which will quench the fiery darts of evil, and 1 Thessalonians 5:19 admonishes us to not put out the fire of the Holy Spirit. In both verses we have the power to quench flames; the flame of evil and the flame of the Holy Spirit. However, in both cases it is our 'agape' love for God that seems to be the overcoming force. 'Agape' keeps the flame of the Spirit alive and 'agape' is the force, which provides us with the faith that is capable of destroying the flame of evil. So the question is, what do we love? It is not possible to resist evil if we love sin. Therefore, our love of sin can and will allow the devil's flame to destroy our faith. It is also only possible to be empowered by the Spirit if we love Christ. Therefore, it is our love for Christ, that enables the Spirit to retain His fire within us. When we have a fully committed love relationship with God, we can withstand the chaos of life and everything else that wants to douse the flame of our spiritual passion. We also need to be reminded that a love that is based solely upon sexual feelings is not true Love Redeemed, because this flame can be put out, and often is.

**Exercise:** Many people express the knowledge that God loves them, but also share that having an emotional love relationship with God is something they have never experienced. One of the reasons that we fail to experience an emotional love relationship with God is that we take for granted the daily gifts of God. Try journaling for a week the many gifts that God has given to you each day. Recognize the things that you take for granted as expressions of God's love towards you: these gifts may be as simple as the breath you breathe or the strength that allows you to get up in the morning.

# Poem 18
# Chastity Valued
# 8:8-10

We have a little sister,
and she has no breasts.
What shall we do for our sister
on the day when she is spoken for?
⁹ If she is a wall,
we will build on her a battlement of silver,
but if she is a door,
we will enclose her with boards of cedar.
¹⁰ I was a wall,
and my breasts were like towers;
then I was in his eyes
as one who finds peace.

This poem is all about the protection of a sister whom her brothers see as not yet physically mature enough to be involved in a relationship. Therefore, they make the claim that if she remains chaste, like a wall, then they will help to protect her innocence. The battlement of silver refers to honor. On the other hand, if she is a door, they will still seek to protect her, but not with honor and not with the same effort, since she has now lost her innocence and honor. The door allows people to pass through the protection of the wall, so the door metaphor suggests that she has been sexually promiscuous. Boarding up a door with cedar is less ambitious than building a silver battlement around her. The silver battlement has a sense of chivalry, honor and the power of protection. The cedar board has a sense of due diligence, but the damage has already been done, and there is no honor in protecting a wall that has already been breached.

Between verses 9 and 10, it seems that some time has passed. The ESV places verse 10 in the past tense, whereas the NIV and NLT choose to use present tense. Either way, I believe that the message is the same: the sister has now matured, and expresses the fact that she is or has been chaste, and therefore there will be no scandal or family embarrassment. As a result of her chastity, she is 'shalom' in her husband's eyes. 'Shalom' means more than peace; the word also encompasses the idea of fulfillment, God's blessings and all that is good and right.

## Marriage Application:

The obvious application is that Love Redeemed calls for sexual purity before marriage. God's desire is that sexual intimacy be awakened only after marriage, and that before marriage; chastity should be protected as something honorable. If you entered marriage as a non-virgin, obviously there is nothing that you can do to change this situation, so it is time to move forward in your relationship. Practice forgiveness of yourself or your spouse, and seek to focus on purity in the current status of your relationship. However, if you are reading this and not married, but you are sexually active with your partner, then you need to consider God's value of chastity.

**Exercise:** If you are not married, but sexually active, this is a good time to discuss ways in which you can correct your lifestyle so as to honor God's value of chastity. If you are married, consider ways in which you can instill the value of chastity into the lives of your children. Most of the media messages that your children receive tell them that it is abnormal to remain a virgin until marriage. Consider what practical ways you can effectively use as a parent to combat this message. At an appropriate age, it is valuable to speak to your children about the beauty of sexual intimacy within God's boundaries. Be careful that your language does not suggest that sex is bad, but then, expect your children to reverse this message after they marry. It is important that they receive the message that sex is beautiful, but God has intended it to be a part of a life-long, committed marriage relationship.

## Allegorical Thought:

Purity always has a role in our relationship with God. The very first commandment that God gave to his people was to have no other gods before him (Exodus 20:3-6). Purity before God requires faithfulness and devotion to the one and only true God. The question we need to ask ourselves on a regular basis is, "Are we keeping faithful to God?" It is important that we don't open ourselves up to situations that allow Satan and his gods the opportunity to invade our lives. A quick examination of how we spend our hours outside of work and sleep will give us some good insight into this area of our spiritual life. Galatians 5:16-26 describes a relationship with the Spirit that is pure. This passage also tells us that other gods can contaminate our relationship with Him.

**Exercise:** Impurity can be defined as the things we know we should not do, but choose to do anyway because it feels good. Spend some time alone with God, and ask him to reveal to you if there are any areas in your life that are impure. Are there areas in your life that you know are wrong, but that you are justifying in spite of your conscience? If God reveals something to you, then seek forgiveness and begin to make the proper changes. Romans 12:2 tells us to stop being conformed to the world and to start changing through the process of renewing our minds. We practice this verse when we stop justifying actions that we know are dishonoring to God.

# POEM 19
# MONOGAMY VALUED
# 8:11-12

Solomon had a vineyard at Baal-hamon;
he let out the vineyard to keepers;
each one was to bring for its fruit a
thousand pieces of silver.
¹² My vineyard, my very own, is before me;
you, O Solomon, may have the thousand,
and the keepers of the fruit two hundred.

In this poem is a word play comparing the actual vineyards of King Solomon to his metaphorical vineyards, which are his wives and concubines. The poem speaks to the inappropriateness of King Solomon using marriage for political and financial gain instead of for God's intended purposes. Love Redeemed leaves no room for marriage to be used as a political maneuver, even if the end goal is peace between two countries.

Metaphorically speaking, vineyards throughout the Song of Songs represent sexual maturity or puberty, and sexual arousal (1:6 & 2:15, 7:12). In this case, the vineyard, as in 1:6, refers to the woman's body. King Solomon had 700 wives and 300 concubines, which adds up to the one thousand pieces of silver mentioned in verse 11. Each wife and concubine was at some time called upon to bring her fruit or sexual pleasures to King Solomon. In verse 12, the woman responds to King Solomon with a statement that could easily be summarized as, "King Solomon may have his 1000 vineyards, but I have one vineyard to call my own, and I am not offering it to the king." The guards or keepers of the fruit would likely be the staff that King Solomon hired to protect his harem, and keep it in top physical condition. Possibly he had 200 of these workers, likely eunuchs, looking after his harem.

The message of this poem is that a woman's vineyard is not an entitlement of the king, even if the king is her own husband. God provides each woman with the right to maintain ownership over her own body. In other words, she is the one who decides when to open the garden gate and when to invite her beloved in. (See comments on poem 11 part B, chapter 4:16)

**Marriage Application:**

I see this poem as speaking to a number of issues: First, a marriage is to be between one man and one woman. The idea of multiple wives was never part of God's original plan. Some may argue that God allowed multiple marriages in the Old Testament. However, when we study the writings of the New Testament, which are the writings of those who lived in the time of Jesus' redemption, it is clear that the church supported only monogamous relationships.

Secondly, with regard to the keepers of the vineyard, marriages need to be exclusive and separate from outside influences. By encouraging the husband to leave his parents and cling to his wife, God has assigned the couple a responsibility for their own relationship without the interference of parents or any other third party. It is not wrong for a couple to seek outside advice, but ultimately they need to choose for themselves how they are going to live their lives and how they will structure their household.

Finally, wives are not the property of their husbands. The concept of submission is not a license to remove freedom of choice. Wives are to be respected as treasured gifts, which have the keys to their own vineyard or garden gate. In 1 Corinthians 7:3-5, Paul states that the wife has authority over her husband's body and the husband has authority over his wife's body, but the context is clear that both need to offer themselves willingly to each other. Paul is not giving permission for a husband or a wife to demand sexual favors from each other, but instead he encourages equal submission. In a healthy marriage, refusing or choosing to have sexual intimacy should be a mutual decision, not the choice of one over the other. However, partners in a healthy marriage will also consider and respect the needs and desires of each other. A loving spouse will not force sex on a partner who is physically or emotionally unable to participate willingly, nor will a loving spouse easily refuse a partner who desires sexual intimacy.

**Exercise:** If you are not having sexual intimacy on a regular basis, this is a yellow flag in your relationship that needs to be addressed. God has designed sexual intimacy for a variety of purposes; one of those purposes is to keep couples closely connected to each other in a physical and emotional way. Take the time to discuss with your partner ways in which you can enjoy sexual intimacy together no less than once a week. Maybe this will require shuffling schedules to fit sexual activity into a busy life or it may mean that you do more to assist each other with household chores so that one of you is not too tired at the end of the day. It may also require that one or both of you receive medical or marital counsel to help you increase your sex drive. There are also some very good Christian blogs on the internet that offer excellent counsel in this area.

**Allegorical Thought:**

In Matthew 23, Jesus gives seven 'woes' to the teachers and religious leaders, admonishing them for their corruption of the spiritual order, which God had put in place for his people. Just like King Solomon's use of marriage, religion had fallen far short of God's expectations, being used by the religious leaders of the day for the purpose of selfish gain, rather than for connecting Israel to God in a pure relationship. It is always a good idea for you to examine your own motives when it comes to attending church and your involvement in functions related to the church. Do you have a selfish reason that is different from God's intent? Are you attending for the value of pretense, which in turn gives you a false sense of significance or purpose? If you truly examine your life with these questions in mind, it is quite likely that you will find that part of your religious practices need to be re-aligned with God's intent when it comes to worship, serving or other spiritual disciplines.

**Exercise:** Take the time this week to examine your spiritual practices. Ask the question, "Why do I do what I do?" Are you 'doing religion' for improper motives, or are the spiritual exercises that you are involved in motivated by your love for Christ? Begin by exploring the areas of church that annoy you the most. This is the area in which you are most likely to discover a misalignment in your thinking.

# POEM 20
# GOD'S FINAL COMMENT
# 8:13-14

O you who dwell in the gardens,
with companions listening for your voice;
let me hear it.
[14] Make haste, my beloved,
and be like a gazelle
or a young stag
on the mountains of spices

The ESV attributes the opening statement of this poem to the voice of the man, but I believe it is the voice of God who is summarizing the message of Love Redeemed in this beautiful Song of Songs. Verse 13 states that the one who is speaking wants to overhear the couples who are dwelling in their garden. Only God has the rightful privilege to listen in on couples enjoying the garden of love. Throughout the Song of Songs, the garden has represented the place where the couple enjoys pure but liberated sexual intimacy with each other. It is the place where they praise each other and offer sexual delights to one another, and since pure sexual intimacy is a metaphor of the glorious relationship that God wants to share with his redeemed people, it also seems appropriate for couples to invite God into their sacred time together. The final song indicates that God desires to be a part of all aspects of a marriage relationship, and that He has a special delight when married couples are experiencing the great joy He has to offer them through sexual intimacy.

Verse 14 is the woman's response to her beloved. It is counter-cultural to have her extending the invitation, but it is also the church's response to its Savior. So, in the final song, as in the first song, she, once again, invites him to hurry to her for the purpose of engaging in sexual joy and passion. In this strange way, we have now come full circle, as this poem could easily continue on with verse 2 of chapter 1 where the Song of all Songs began with her inviting her beloved to kiss her and run away with her into his bed chamber.

**Marriage Application:**

God permits, and in fact, encourages couples to experience the fullness of sexual intimacy with each other. We need to be reminded that sex is God's creation, to be enjoyed and not to be abused. Sexual intimacy can also be a reminder to us of the day when we will experience the new Eden of heaven that God is preparing for us. So, in light of what we have learned, and in response to the final verse, "Couples, make haste. What are you waiting for?" Love has been redeemed.

**Exercise:** What are you waiting for? Go! Make haste! Enjoy the sexual intimacy of marriage that God has gifted to you.

**Allegorical Thought:**

It is exciting to acknowledge that, in a strange and mysterious way, we can have a relationship with God that is equally as pleasurable as 'Eros' love between a husband and wife. As we continue on our spiritual journey, it is important for us to longingly seek out this relationship. If this has not been your experience, then in the same way as the gazelles of the field, you also need to hasten into a closer experience with God. It is my desire that some of the thoughts and exercises presented through this study will help you to do just that.

**Exercise:** Make haste to draw closer into a love relationship with the One who has redeemed your soul and who has set you free to enjoy and express a reconciled relationship between you and God.

# APPENDIX

In the 'Allegorical Thought' exercises of a couple of the poems, I recommended spending time with God in a way that allows you to awaken the five senses that He has given to you. The following is a prayer retreat that I have put together for the purpose of helping you to focus with your senses on the presence of God around you. Feel free to use part or all of these retreat ideas as you seek to accomplish the exercise of drawing closer to God through sight, sound, taste, touch and smell.

Part of drawing close to God is the realization that creation is not something that God did and then separated himself. In other words, He is not just sitting back letting the world spin without paying any attention to it. God could have designed our world in this way, but He didn't. God is intricately involved in every aspect of our world, in the same way that a juggler is totally focused on all of the balls that are in the air. If God turned away for just one moment, the whole world would collapse. He is actually a part of every breath that you take. If God were absent, we would not exist.

When we were younger, we experienced times when our teacher or parents told us to pay attention. During these times, we had to force our minds and ears to listen and seek to comprehend the message that was being given to us. The person in authority was asking us to stop daydreaming and to focus on learning. Paying attention to God, however, is different. God shows up in our daydream, and our responsibility is to notice him. God has given us our senses of sight, smell, touch, sound and taste. These are all tools of blessing, which help us to experience God's presence: so pay attention to all of your senses! We have all experienced moments in life when the things around us, such as a beautiful scenic place, or a magnificent achievement have fascinated us. These are the times when we have been attentive to what we see. God speaks into our lives at these moments to remind us that He has been involved. God shows up as the power and creative mind behind what we see. Recognition of this leads us to praise, which is prayer.

There have also been times when we have seen things that have disturbed us, times of destruction and ugliness that have moved us to compassion, maybe even to anger or tears. Examples of these difficult moments may include our awareness or experience of such things as homelessness, poverty, injustice, natural disasters, pain and suffering or abuse. During these times, God also shows up. God is loving and compassionate, and so He shows up in the outpouring of our sadness. We feel what He feels, which allows us to experience God through our emotions. The Spirit of God speaks to us through our desire to reach out and help.

There are also moments in life when we are in a relationship, either with an individual or a community, which allows us to enjoy just being ourselves and accepting others for who they are. During these times, when laughter and feelings of joy are part of everyone's experience. God is also in these moments because he has designed us for relationship and community.

Finally, God is also in the community when we struggle with seeking to find solutions to problems, or when we're sweating together on a work project, or when we are grieving the loss of a community member. All of these are times when God is equally present, and it is our job to acknowledge him through praise or guidance or comfort or perseverance or whatever response is appropriate. It is always our task to pay attention to God around us. Note: paying attention is all about what is happening in the present moment not the past or the future. Prayer is recognizing the God who is in the present, and it is during these times of awareness that the Spirit of God, who indwells our body, speaks to us of God's goodness and grace.

**Our Senses:**

God has provided us with 5 senses by which we are allowed to experience His creation and consequently, Himself. These are the senses of sight, hearing, smelling, tasting and touching. For this prayer retreat we are going to practice awakening those senses so that we can experience God more closely in our lives. **There are some items that you will need to bring with you, so before launching on your retreat, please read through the following section and take note of the items to bring with you. They are listed at the beginning of each sense.**

**Eyes – the sense of seeing**

Bring along something to take pictures with. (If it is a cell phone, leave it shut off except for the exercise of taking pictures.) You may also want to bring something that plays music. I have listed a few songs below that you may want to download or collect before the retreat.

Note: these are just my suggestions: you may have other preferences.

Begin by singing a few songs that speak about the eyes and the heart. The following are a few suggestions:

- Open the eyes of my heart Lord – I want to see Jesus (by Michael W. Smith)
- Open my eyes Lord I want to see Jesus – (author unknown)
- Open my eyes, that I may see – (by Clara H. Scott)
- Be Thou My Vision – (by Dallan Forgaill)

The following are some Scripture passages to consider: Ephesians 1:15-23, Psalm 119:18, Psalm 27:13, 66:1-5.

Once you have sung a couple of songs and have read the above Scripture passages, open your Bible to the story in John chapter 9. Read this story and imagine yourself as the blind man. Ask yourself the following questions:

- What is it that you need to do in order to prepare your mind and heart to be open to what God desires to show you today?
- Spend some time asking God to remove whatever Spiritual blindness may be in your life today. "Search me, O God, and know my heart!"

**Exercise 2:**

Using your camera, cell phone or tablet, pencil & paper – (any device that captures pictures), go for a walk with God and seek out His beauty by taking pictures. Look for the intricate design in creation, as well as the vastness of His creation. Look for obvious beauty and strange beauty. With each photo/picture give praise to God and ask him what he wants to say to you about Himself.

**Mouth – the sense of taste**

I would recommend trying this as your lunchtime experience.

Psalm 34:8 "Taste & See that the Lord is Good"

Pack the following for a lunchtime experience: 1 bottle of water, 1 small grape juice, baggy of raw vegetables and fruit (Make sure you include something like radishes or a small container of horse radish. Also include some dried figs.), 1 or 2 bun/s, slices of cold meat such as ham, if possible some cold lamb.

Before eating each item, you will be encouraged to reflect and then make the statement "taste and see that the Lord is good". I would encourage you to follow the format as laid out below.

- Various fruits & vegetables (Read: Genesis 2:15-17)
  - Reflection: Imagine all of the different fruits and vegetables that we have in our world. God gave every one of them to you for your benefit and enjoyment. Share your favorite fruit and vegetables with the group. In the same way that you might offer a toast at a wedding, hold up a fruit or vegetable and say, *"taste and see that the Lord is good."*
- Bitter herbs - Radish or horse radish (Read: Exodus 12:8, Numbers 9:11)
  - Reflection: Not everything is good to the taste. During the Passover meal, the people were

required to eat bitter herbs as a reminder of the difficult years in Egypt.
  - ➢ During those difficult years, God continued to have his eye on his people. Sometimes we might have difficult seasons in life that are hard to bear. Eat some of the bitter herbs as a reminder that God watches over us even through the tough times. Before you eat (in the same way that you might offer a toast at a wedding), hold up a bitter herb and say *"taste and see that the Lord is good."*
- Water – (Read: John 7:37-39, 4:7-15)
  - ➢ Reflection: After eating those bitter herbs, you may be desperate to drink some water. Psalm 42:1 reads, "As the deer pants for streams of water, so my soul pants for you, my God. My soul thirsts for God, for the living God."
  - ➢ Jesus tells us that He is the living water, and that the water he gives to us will be like a spring of life bubbling up inside of us. Before you drink (in the same way that you might offer a toast at a wedding), hold up your water and say, *"taste and see that the Lord is good."*
- Bread – (Read: John 6:27-40)
  - ➢ Reflection: God fed the people in the wilderness with manna and Jesus feeds us spiritually with the bread of life, which he reminds us is his body. Just like the living water will never allow you to go thirsty, so the living bread will never allow you to go hungry. Before you eat (in the same way that you might offer a toast at a wedding), hold up your bread and say, *"taste and see that the Lord is good."*

- Meat - lamb (Read: Genesis 22:7-8, John 1:29, Isaiah 53:7, Rev.5:6-10)
  - ➤ Reflection: As you read through the Scripture selections you will notice the question in Genesis "Where is the lamb?" The remainder of the verses provide us with the answer. As we eat of the lamb, let us remember that the sacrificial lamb has been slain for the atonement of many. Before you eat (in the same way that you might offer a toast at a wedding), hold up your lamb and say, *"taste and see that the Lord is good."*
- Meat – pork (Read: Acts10:9-16)
  - ➤ Reflection: Pork is a reminder that the good news of the gospel has also been given to non-Jews. As Gentiles, we are able to experience the benefits of God's chosen people. Salvation has come to us. Before you eat (in the same way that you might offer a toast at a wedding), hold up your ham and say, *"taste and see that the Lord is good."*
- Grape juice/wine – (Read: Luke 22:17-20)
  - ➤ The fruit of the vine is an important metaphor throughout Scripture. In this passage, it reminds us of the covenant that Jesus has made with us through His blood.
  - ➤ Jesus also allows us to reflect on the end of time when all of his followers will be gathered together to enjoy the cup with him. Before you drink (in the same way that you might offer a toast at a wedding), hold up your juice and say, *"taste and see that the Lord is good."*
- Figs (Read: Luke 21:29-33, Jeremiah 24)

> Figs in Scripture can be related to blessings from God or curses if the figs are bad or non-existent.
> Vs.6-7 reminds us that God is watching over us, that He will build us up, and give us a heart to know and desire God, so that we will be His people and He will be our God. What an amazing promise! Before you eat (in the same way that you might offer a toast at a wedding), hold up your figs and say, *"taste and see that the Lord is good."*

Take some time now to thank God for his bountiful blessings, and then to enjoy the rest of your meal in fellowship.

**Afternoon**

**Body – the sense of touch**

In a backpack, bring with you some of your favorite things to touch and a notebook. Also, include an envelope with some nails and some thorns (possibly from a rose bush or raspberry bush).

Find a patch of grass to sit down on.

Thoughts – The Lord is my Shepherd – he leads me to lie down in green pastures

Imagine that you are a sheep lying in a patch of green grass. Enjoy the feeling of being one of his sheep. How does it feel to know that you are under the care and protection of the great shepherd? With eyes closed, quote the 23rd Psalm.

**Exercise:** In your notebook, write down all of the pleasant touches that you have experienced. As you write them down, imagine what they feel like and thank God for the experience. This is the time that you might want to handle the items that you brought with you. As you are imagining the touch of items, don't forget to include things like hot and cold, soft and hard, etc.

Now shift gears. The Bible tells us that we will one day have no pain or tears because Jesus took our pain. Imagine a world without pain. Take out the package that includes nails and thorns. Read Isaiah 53. Try to imagine what it was like for Jesus.

- the pain of rejection,
- the whips
- the crown of thorns
- Ultimately the cross.

Allow yourself to experience the love of Jesus who suffered the pain of touch on your behalf. Now give Him all of your aches, heartaches, disappointments, pains, and anxieties. Allow Jesus to bear those pains on your behalf.

**Nose – the sense of smell**

Scripture Passages to Read: 2 Corinthians 2:14-17, Ephesians 5:2, Philippians 4:18 Exodus 30:34-38, John 12:3

Aroma and fragrance in the above passages are all gifts. Some are gifts to God, while other fragrances are the gift we offer to others. Take some time to go for a walk and enjoy the fragrances in the air. Allow these fragrances to remind you of God's blessings to you. Now spend some time in quietness before God and allow God to speak to you of your gift of fragrance towards others. In what way are you a blessing to those around you?

**Ears – the sense of hearing**

Scripture Passages to Read: Isa.34:1-2, 50:4-5, Psalm 28:1-2, 61, 66:16-20, 98

Thoughts – this could be the last sense of the day. If you brought some worship music with you, then you could play that or you may just want to sit in the quietness of nature and take note of the sounds that are around you. How has God spoken to you today? This is the time to journal about the message that God wants you to receive today.

# BIBLIOGRAPHY

Cole, Philip D. *Discovering A More Intimate Response.* Denver: Outskirts Press, 2014.

Ethridge, Shannon *The Passion Principles.* Nashville: W Publishing Group, 2014.

Hess, Richard S. *Song of Songs.* Baker Commentary on the Old Testament Wisdom and Psalms. Grand Rapids: Baker Academic, 2005

Klassen, Randolph J. *Meditations For Lovers.* Chicago: Covenant Press.

Longman, Tremper III. *The Song of Songs.* New International Commentary on the Old Testament. Grand Rapids: Eerdmans, 2001.

Longman, Tremper III. *Song of Songs.* Cornerstone Biblical Commentary. Carol Stream: Tyndale House Publishers, Inc., 2006.

Provan, Iain *Ecclesiastes/Song of Songs.* The NIV Application Commentary. Grand Rapids: Zondervan, 2001.

Ryken, Leland, Wilhoit, James C., Longman, Tremper III gen ed. *The Dictionary of Biblical Imagery.* Downers Grove: Inter Varsity Press, 1998.